James Stephen Jeans

Trusts, Pools and Corners as Affecting Commerce and Industry

James Stephen Jeans

Trusts, Pools and Corners as Affecting Commerce and Industry

ISBN/EAN: 9783337366209

Printed in Europe, USA, Canada, Australia, Japan

Cover: Foto ©Suzi / pixelio.de

More available books at **www.hansebooks.com**

TRUSTS
POOLS AND CORNERS

AS AFFECTING COMMERCE AND INDUSTRY

An Inquiry

INTO THE PRINCIPLES AND RECENT OPERATION OF
COMBINATIONS AND SYNDICATES TO LIMIT
PRODUCTION AND INCREASE PRICES

BY

J. STEPHEN JEANS, M.R.I., F.S.S.

AUTHOR OF

"ENGLAND'S SUPREMACY," "RAILWAY PROBLEMS," ETC.

Methuen & Co.

36 ESSEX STREET, LONDON, W.C.

1894

PREFATORY NOTE

In the following pages, the word "Trust" has been uniformly employed to signify combinations of every kind that have been devised with a view to controlling production and prices. There may be other words that more correctly express the exact character of the principles upon which certain combinations are founded, and the objects they have in view. But, however much the appellation may be entitled to the description of a mere euphemism, and however much it may fall short of the better known English term "Ring," in conveying an adequate idea of the methods employed and the ends in view, it is the word commonly used in the United States to describe such combinations, and is not perhaps so offensive to those who may honestly approve of those principles and ends, apart from considerations of mere expediency.

Exception may be taken to the fact that in the following pages I have not pronounced very definite approval or condemnation of the Trust system generally, but I do not consider that I am called upon to do so. I am neither their apologist nor their judge. My function has been to present, as far as I could, within the limits at my disposal, the facts as to their character, operations, and development, and this I have endeavoured to do without conscious partiality or prejudice. The system is neither wholly good nor wholly evil, and he who would strongly pronounce it to be necessarily either, is likely to err in his judgment.

                                        J. STEPHEN JEANS.

GREAT GEORGE STREET, LONDON, S.W.
        March 1894.

CONTENTS

CONTENTS

TRUSTS, POOLS AND CORNERS.

CHAPTER I.

THE purpose of this volume is that of considering and dealing with the whole question of artificial restraints upon trade. The natural course of trade tends to establish a system of free and unfettered competition in every direction, and experience has proved that this system of competition, if left entirely to itself, may easily do great mischief, not, indeed, to the general public, but to the competitors themselves. Much depends upon whether the competition is what is known as fair and above-board competition, or whether it is carried on with poisoned weapons and loaded dice. The competition that was carried on a number of years ago among the principal railway companies having London termini was unfair and disastrous as between the companies concerned. So violent did the rivalry become, that passengers were carried at much less than the cost of transport, and it is even stated that in certain cases people were offered other inducements to travel by particular lines. On the other hand, the competition now carried on between rival railway companies converging on the same points,

A

although as keen as ever, is usually strictly fair and reasonable, being a competition in inducements and facilities that are not of the cut-throat character previously practised. The companies concerned now generally agree to charge the same fares or rates from common points to common points, instead of underbidding each other in a way that was calculated to prove only who had the longest purse and the greatest powers of endurance.

The system of cutting rates or prices may answer for a time, but in the long run it is likely to recoil upon the heads of those who commence it. Indeed, it is usually the poorest and the least capable who are the most reckless, so long as the game lasts, and that for the very simple and intelligible reason that they have the least to lose. The stronger rivals, on the other hand, can hardly hope to gain much, if anything, by playing at the reckless game of beggar-my-neighbour. If it were merely competition between rival groceries or dry-goods houses, it might partially succeed, if the weakest were absolutely driven into bankruptcy, although even then it is by no means certain that there would not be a resurrection of the defunct business. But, as applied to manufacturing or transportation enterprise, such manœuvres are practically certain to defeat their own end. A railway, once built, is difficult to get rid of. A manufactory, a mine, a blast furnace, a steel-works, or any similar establishment may, indeed, be driven into bankruptcy, but that is all. By and bye, phœnix-like, it will rise from its ashes, perhaps to "nobler things," and the undercutting rival is denied the reaping of the harvest for which the seeds had been so diligently sown. Often it is found that, with a greatly reduced capital, consequent upon having been "picked up cheap" by new owners, the weaker becomes the stronger, and the expectations on which the price-cutting policy was founded become sadly blighted. Competition, therefore, pursued to the bitter end is not wholesome for those who engage in it, and it is desirable that some checks should be interposed to the usual consequence of competition—the unwholesome process of having the lean kine swallowed up by the fat, as in the Biblical legend.

The history of manufacturing industry is a record of ups and downs—of alternate prosperity and depression—according as the supply is above or below the demand. The enormous development that has taken place of late years in the facilities for production and distribution have tended to create gluts that were almost unknown half a century ago. In every industry, almost without exception, processes and appliances have been so perfected, that the means of production have been multiplied many-fold. The same investment of capital, and the same application of labour, will now produce infinitely more, by the aid of machinery of the most perfect and approved type, than it would have done only a few years ago. A modern blast furnace will yield over 2000 tons of pig-iron per week, under favourable conditions, where probably less than a hundred tons was the rule half a century ago. A modern cotton factory will show a couple of thousand spindles being "minded" by two operatives, and working at the rate of nearly 10,000 revolutions per minute, where such results would have been deemed impossible not many years ago. Simultaneously with this enormous advance in the resources of production, there has been a notable increase in the proportion of the population of the principal industrial countries engaged in manufactures. In our own and other countries, the recent tendency of population is to forsake the country and swell the towns—to abandon agriculture in favour of manufactures. Everything, indeed, has tended to the increase of manufactures, and that being so, it is not perhaps a matter of wonder that unlimited means of production are usually face to face with a limited consumption.

The natural result of this state of things is a frequent " glut," and periodical depression of a more or less intense and universal character. The constant effort and aim of producers is to secure riches by manufacturing and selling cheaper than their neighbours. A maxim that appears to govern all modern manufacturing operations is that the cheapest and best system to adopt is that of production on a large scale, and when all alike are striving with might and main for this result, it becomes easy for production to overtake the demand. In a general way, the remedy hitherto applied for over-production has been to reduce the quantity produced. Hence it often happens that the manufacturing resources of an industrial country are seldom fully employed. In the iron trade, it rarely happens that more than one-half of the blast furnaces built are engaged in making pig-iron. The same remark applies, *mutatis mutandis*, to many other industries. The United States, for example, are possessed of resources for the manufacture of both iron and steel far in excess of what they actually require, and their present plant is estimated to be equal to turning out nearly as much again of both as they produced in 1891. A large capital is thus continually unproductive, and the profits that should accrue in respect of this capital are either entirely lost, or have to be earned from that part of the plant that is found in work.

On the other hand, it is obvious that when supply is so

generally and so largely in excess of the demand—when an unlimited production is constantly brought in line with a limited consumption—prices must tend downwards, until they reach the point at which only the most favourably-equipped establishments can work at a profit, while the less favourably-placed producers must go to the wall. If the evil stopped here, there would be less to complain of. But a factory or a workshop, a blast furnace or a rolling mill, a mine or a quarry, once set in motion, has come to stay. As we have seen, original owners may succumb to the law which decrees the survival of the fittest; but the establishment usually changes hands at much less than its original cost, and then resumes the contest with more enterprise than ever. The consequences are often disastrous, and the blanks are much more numerous than the prizes; but the hopes that are inspired by the knowledge of the exceptional experience of the few, induce the many to continue the struggle. It is calculated by one of the principal coal-owners in the Great Northern Coal-field, that the average profits made in that industry over the last thirty years have not exceeded 3 per cent. In the Cotton trade the average profits over the same period have been estimated at barely $3\frac{1}{2}$ per cent. In many trades the average profits have been much less even than these. Much is made of the few who, from special circumstances, have reaped large rewards. Of the many whose faces are turned to the wall little or nothing is known. The fierce light of publicity beats upon exceptional prosperity. Adversity, on the contrary, is retiring and reserved.

The ingenuity and perseverance of mankind have, for the last thirty years, been as earnestly and laboriously directed to the work of finding a remedy for low prices and irregular

demand, as they were in a former age to the discovery of
that fabled alembic which was credited with the power of
transmuting all the baser metals into gold. Needless to say,
they have not been successful in their endeavours. The
remedial measures possible are, in truth, extremely few and
simple. Besides the obviously natural and rational cure of
keeping down production until it has been overtaken by
demand, the only specifics that have hitherto been devised
by the wit of man are Customs' tariffs, which keep out
imports, and combinations of capitalists designed to secure
a virtual control of the resources of production or of distribution, as the case may be.

It is the latter remedy—the attempt to regulate and control the operations of supply—that we are here specially
concerned with. The natural effect of establishing in any
industry a syndicate or combination strong enough to
regulate the supply must be to advance prices. The
advance may not be, and seldom is, a large one. But in
these days, when profits are calculated to a fourth and fifth
place in decimals of one per cent., a very fractional advance
may make all the difference between a fair profit and a considerable loss.

Manifestly, combination so established interferes with
the free play of competition, and it is therefore denounced
as being in restraint of trade. The capitalist or producer
seldom meets with much sympathy whatever his reverses
may be. If his troubles ultimately overwhelm him, he is
told that he should have gone into something else, or done
some impossible thing differently. "Let us take care
of the consumer," is the shibboleth of the modern economist; "the producer can look after himself."

Under these circumstances the individual producer suffers

in order that the great body of consumers may gain. Every-thing that the State or society may legally and fairly do in order to encourage competition is done. No doubt, on the whole, this system is just and salutary. But under our present industrial methods it leads to frequent unfortunate results. Exports and imports fluctuate seriously as between one year and another. No equilibrium between supply and demand is possible. When a "boom" is on, production is strained to the utmost. When the reaction comes, factories are closed, furnaces are damped down, operatives are thrown out of employment by hundreds and thousands, wives and families fall victims to starvation, employers pass through the bankruptcy court, the poor rates become swollen, and a whole legion of other evils are entailed. Most truly, if competition is the lesser of the two evils, it is still an evil of serious magnitude.

During the last few years the disposition to regulate com-petition has probably been manifested over a wide area, and has shown much more energy than it had previously done. Some of its developments will be traced in the pages that follow. But it may at once and for all be affirmed that no combination is likely to be of much avail against the mani-fold evils of unbridled competition, unless it obtains the virtual control of the commodity that is over-produced. Such control is obviously liable to great abuse. There is a danger lest a combination, established for a per-fectly legitimate purpose, should drift into tyrannical monopoly; and monopolies, as we have elsewhere shown (p. 15), are dangerous to society. On the whole, then, it would seem as if free competition were the safer alternative. It has many drawbacks, and is attended with not a few evils, but it secures an ample supply of commodities at a cheap price, and that is the great desideratum after all.

"Every European government," says Buckle,* "which has legislated respecting trade, has acted as if its main object were to suppress the trade and ruin the traders. Instead of leaving the national industry to take its own course, it has been troubled by an interminable series of regulations, all intended for its good, and all inflicting serious harm. To such a height has this been carried that the commercial reforms which have distinguished England during the last twenty years have solely consisted in un-doing this mischievous and intrusive legislation."

There is a danger lest the recent tendency to interfere with trade combinations should reproduce the patriarchal and restraining conditions on which Buckle animadverted. Certain legislative proposals recently under discussion in the United States virtually enacted that no two men can agree on the price at which they will sell any article, that two individuals cannot agree to cease competing in trade, and that no combination which affects prices shall be legal. Such enactments, it has been truly observed, not only tend to destroy all partnerships, all corporations, all aggregations of capital, all unity of effort in business, all compromises by which the disasters of over-competition are frequently asserted, but would simply render business impossible.†

The original idea of a syndicate or trust appears to have been that producers should come to an understanding among themselves as to how much each should produce, and what common price should be charged to the public.

* Vol. i. p. 277.
† "Combinations: their Uses and Abuses." By S. C. T. Dodd. New York, 1888.

Each producer, however, was left with absolute control over his own business in other respects.

On the face of it, this would appear to be the most natural and satisfactory arrangement for all parties. And so, indeed, it would have been if all alike had been equally loyal and trustworthy. But it was found difficult to keep all the parties to such a compact true to the spirit as well as the letter of the bond. The combination suffered, in not a few cases, from the bad faith of its individual members, some of whom either undersold the combination rate or produced quantities in excess of that provided for by regulation.

It was for the purpose of avoiding such possible acts of bad faith on the part of the individual members of a combination that the American institution, known as a trust, was established. The fundamental idea of a trust is that the affairs of all its individual members shall be absolutely controlled by the organisation and for the organisation. In order to do this, of course, it is necessary that the trust shall do more than merely control production and price, although that may be, and generally is, the sole *raison d'être* of the combination. The trust must be the virtual if not the absolute owner of all the properties or concerns that are parties to the compact. This is usually achieved by buying out all the different works or other properties that are engaged in the business which it is proposed to control. A large capital is usually necessary for the purpose, but it often happens that the proprietors of the concerns syndicated are content to accept their payment in trust shares. This was the case with the Salt Trust and the Chemical Trust in England, to which, in each case, all the principal producers were parties. It was not the case with the copper mine owners, who were simply controlled as to production and price, and this, in all probability, was one of the chief causes of the failure of the Copper Syndicate. The general form of the trust or syndicate is, however, that of a combination of producers to keep up prices. Such have been the trusts generally established in the United States, and it is the form assumed by combination in the steel rail and other industries.

A syndicate may be formed on many different lines, and the arrangements made or proposed for the realisation of its leading aim are legion, including the following as the chief types :—

1. It may absolutely purchase all the properties proposed to be syndicated, and thereby absolutely control the whole of the possible production of the commodity for the time being.

2. It may arrange with producers, under penalties for breach of contract, as to the quantities of the commodities to be produced by each, and the prices at which the commodity shall be sold, as in the case of the so-called " vend " in the coal trade of the north of England.

3. It may undertake, without purchase of the properties, or exercising other control over them, to purchase and to sell at its own price all the produce of particular mines or works, as in the case of the *Société des Metaux*.

4. It may take the form of an arrangement among producers to fix the proportions of the whole output to be contributed by each, and the uniform price at which that output shall be sold, leaving each concern perfect freedom in

> dealing with its own customers within these limitations.
>
> 5. It may, in addition to these provisions, arrange to "pool" all the orders that come into the market.

The operations of rings, pools, and syndicates are generally founded on the principle that it is desirable to limit the quantity of the given commodity to be regulated, and is in direct opposition to the axiom of Bastiat, that "the riches of men consist in the abundance of things." This axiom is, of course, referring to abundance in its widest signification, for the individual is no doubt favourably affected by scarcity. The seller is generally anxious that there should be a limited supply in his own particular line, and scarcity is his *beau ideal* of what is good—for himself.

In exposing the fallacies which underlie the pretexts for protection, Bastiat laid down the following aphorisms, which are fully as applicable to artificial attempts to create scarcity by operations of which the Salt Syndicate in England and the Copper Syndicate in France are familiar types—

"A radical antagonism exists between the seller and the buyer.

"The seller desires that the object should be of limited supply, and therefore scarce and dear.

"The buyer desires it abundant, and therefore cheap.

"The laws, which should be at least neutral, take the part of the seller against the buyer, of the producer against the consumer, of dearness against cheapness, and therefore of scarcity against abundance."

The old laws of England rendered illegal all attempts to artificially reduce the supply, or raise the prices of necessary commodities. The practices so condemned were—

1. *Badgering*, or buying in a market before the regular hour.

2. *Forestalling*, or buying provisions on their way to market.

3. *Engrossing*, or buying to sell again, in or near the same market.

4. *Regrating*, or persuading persons from taking goods to market, and buying goods in large quantities to sell again.

The Act 71, Geo. III., recited that "it hath been found by experience that the restraints laid by several statutes upon the dealing in corn, meal, flour, cattle, and sundry other sort of victuals, by preventing a free trade in the same commodities, have a tendency to discourage the growth and enhance the price of the same;" and consequently the old statutes were repealed. The Act 7 and 8, Vic., swept away forty of these old statutes at one stroke, for the same and kindred reasons. We shall see as we proceed, that the tendency of recent legislation in some countries, and notably in the United States, has been to re-impose such enactments—to restrain the liberty of individuals where its exercise was calculated to interfere with public interests in buying and selling.

Some years ago I wrote, in words which I cannot now alter for the better, and which I am now as much as ever ready to adopt, that "the extraordinary development of the system of establishing syndicates, or pools, or trusts, as they are euphemistically termed, for the purpose of monopolising the supplies of a commodity that is in everyday request, and thereby controlling the price at which it shall be sold to the public, has gone so far during the last year or two that it is not only an unmitigated nuisance, but it threatens to become, if it has not already attained to the proportions of, a grave public danger. In whatever direction we may turn we shall find that attempts have been made, and in only too many cases have been successful, to obtain from the public by the power of capital, allied to good organisation of details, much larger prices than they would have to pay under a system of unrestricted trade, and the natural operation of the laws of supply and demand.

"It is natural enough that the appearance of this new force in our midst should excite apprehension and even alarm. A country like England depends almost for its very existence upon its means of purchasing, at a relatively cheap rate, all the commodities that it consumes. If those means are withdrawn from us, by rings or other combinations that are designed to raise the prices of the raw materials of commerce to the manufacturer, of their food supplies to the people, of manufactured goods to the foreigner, of 'all things to all men,' then, indeed, is England exposed to a risk compared with which our absolute renunciation of our policy of free trade would be but small. The new force— the force of capital and combination acting in concert—is capable of doing infinite mischief. But it is also capable of achieving great good. The object of the economist, the politician, and the social reformer ought, therefore, to be to so control the new force as to minimise its power for evil and increase its power for good."

There can be little doubt that the public conscience has become, within recent years, much less tender than it formerly was as regards the aiding and abetting of syndicated or regulated trade, and even "corners" have been talked of with something very like approval, especially where they have been attended with a reasonable amount of success, the ill-starred fortunes of the copper ring, or *Société des Metaux*, notwithstanding. Men of business integrity and influence have been more ready to ally themselves with such movements than formerly — so much so that the *Saturday Review* recently remarked, and with reason—

"Twenty years ago—ten years ago perhaps, no great merchant or banker could have been found in England willing to risk his good name by association with any such enterprise as a trade ring—none who would have consented to share the profits of any kind of corner. But, apparently, the younger generation have looked upon the prodigious gains of certain American speculators—men who reckon what they jocularly call their 'plunder' by tens of millions sterling—and the spectacle has been too much for some of them. Conscious of all the necessary means of playing the same game—with heaps of capital to sustain it, perfect knowledge of the ins and outs, ample command of every variety of shrewdness and calculation, full facility of combination at home and abroad—it is not wonderful, perhaps, if some of our respectables began to ask themselves why they should not become Jay Goulds too. But inasmuch as they have yielded to the temptation, or are disposed to yield to it, it is a serious matter for the credit and safety of British commerce."

CHAPTER II.

COMBINATIONS REGARDED AS MONOPOLIES.

UNTIL comparatively recent times, monopolies of all kinds were "thick as autumnal leaves in Valambrossa," throughout the world. This was especially true of trade and commerce, which were the surest means of yielding the riches that mankind has always been prone to covet. Before the Christian era, trade had been monopolised by the Oriental kings.* In the middle ages it was usual for trades and industries to be the subjects of monopoly, by individuals who had started them, or by committees that possessed special facilities for carrying them on. Thus, in 1348, all the tin mines in England were monopolised by a German. About the same time the woollen industry was monopolised by the weavers of Lincoln. A century later, the "king's merchants" are said to have monopolised all the known resources in alum, and this monopoly was continued under a patent granted in 1505 by King Henry VII. Among patents granted to committees may be mentioned one for the regulation of rope-making, in the town of Bridport, Dorsetshire, in 1530,† and another limiting the manufacture of cloth to the inhabitants of Worcester, Evesham, Droitwich, Kidderminster, and Bromsgrove, upon the petition of these towns to be relieved from the competi-

* Macpherson's "Annals of Commerce," vol. i. pp. 168, 169, 178.
† 21, Hen. VIII., c. 12.

tion of "divers persons, dwelling in the hamlets, thorps, and villages of the said shire," who had "not only engrossed and taken into their hands sundry farms, and become graziers and husbandmen, but also make all manner of cloths, and exercise weaving, fulling, and shearing within their own houses, to the great depopulation" of the towns named.*

Macpherson † mentions one curious case of a monopoly being granted for the manufacture of coverlets for beds in the city of York, because "sundry *evil-disposed* persons, apprentices, not experts in that occupation, have withdrawn themselves out of the city into the country;" while others made coverlets "neither of good stuff nor proper size," and hawked them abroad, "to the great deceit of the king's subjects." This ordinance, made in 1544, was in 1852 followed by one which secured to the city of Norwich, and to all other corporate or market towns of that county, a monopoly of the manufacture of "felt hats and thrummed hats, coverlets, and dornecks (diaper linen)." ‡

Although it is not the object of the present work to enter at length into the history of manufacturing and commercial monopolies, it is germane to the subject in hand to point out that in course of time they were felt to be a grievous burden, so much so that many attempts were made to restrain or annul them. In 1601, Queen Elizabeth cancelled most of the grants of this description made by previous sovereigns, for which she was awarded the thanks of Parliament, and two years later, King James issued a proclamation ordering the annulment of several flagrant cases of the

* 25, Hen. VIII., c. 18.
† "Annals of Commerce," vol. ii. p. 91.
‡ 5, 6, Edw. VI., c. 24.

same kind. The latter monarch, however, was not consistent in his treatment of the evil. In the next year or two he not only granted many patents securing a monopoly of manufacture or sale to certain favoured persons, but he himself monopolised the manufacture of alum, tobacco, and finished cloth. So intolerable had the evil become in 1609, that the king was obliged to revoke all his monopolies by proclamation. This course had to be repeated again in 1624, when the increasing growth of monopolies was considered by Parliament; and once more, in 1639, the same course had to be repeated. There was, however, this excuse to be made for the monopolies of those days, that they were made a source of revenue for carrying on the government of the country, albeit they were probably used more frequently for gratifying the reigning monarch's extravagant desires.

Akin to the monopolies granted for carrying on manufacturing industry were the patents granted to inventors of processes or appliances for the improvement of manufactures. It has, however, been recognised by all civilised countries, up to the present time, that this is a just and reasonable form of monopoly, and that to withhold it would be prejudicial to the public interest, in so far as it would restrain original research and discovery, and the general application of valuable inventions. One of the first patents named by Macpherson * was granted in 1618 to John Gilbert, for the sole manufacture and sale of an instrument which he called a water plough, and of an engine for draining coal pits and other mines.† When monopolies were swept away wholesale by the royal proclamation of 1624,

* "Annals of Commerce," vol. ii. p. 289.
† Fœdera, V., xvii., p. 102.

the king specially reserved the right to grant patents for fourteen years, "for new invented manufactures or arts, never practised before, and not being mischievous to the State, by raising the prices of commodities at home or the hurt of trade."* This ordinance was really the foundation of our patent laws, as they exist at the present time.

Scarcely less hurtful than monopolies and patents to the free course of industry and commerce was the custom that prevailed in the middle ages, and up to comparatively recent times, of excluding from one country the produce and manufactures of another. This was a common method of punishing the country with which commerce was prohibited, and naturally such restraints led to reprisals. The principal culprits were England and France, but the other nations of Europe were not free from the same absurdly archaic and illogical practices. Thus, for example, we find it stated that, in 1646, Louis XIII. of France ordered "that no kind of grain, wines, or pulse should be exported to England, nor from England to France, nor any cloths, serges, wools, lead, tin, stuffs, silk stockings, &c.—in a word, all commerce between the two countries was wholly prohibited."

But, with or without monopolies, the business of the trader or manufacturer in the middle ages must have been attended with large profits. "The merchants of different countries," says Hallam, "became so opulent as almost to rival the ancient nobility," while "the trading companies possessed either a positive or a virtual monopoly, and held the keys of those Eastern regions for the luxuries of which the progressive refinement of manners produced an in-

* 21, Jac. I., c. 3.

creasing demand." * Money commanded a high rate of interest. At Verona, in 1228, it was fixed at 12½ per cent. At Modena, in 1270, it appears to have been as high as 20 per cent. Philip the Fair, in 1311, allowed 20 per cent. after the first year of the loan. The annual profit made by Venice on her mercantile capital has been reckoned at 40 per cent. In England "commerce now became, next to liberty, the leading subject of Parliament," and from the accession of Edward III. the greater part of our statutes relate to this subject—"not always well devised, or liberal, or consistent, but by no means worse in those respects than such as have been enacted in subsequent ages." †

In modern times the State has only granted monopolies for the public interest, as in the case of a railway, gas or water works, or other organisation in respect of which capital required protection against itself.

The genius of the laws of most civilised countries is against monopoly, where the end in view can be secured without it. The concessions granted in remote, sparsely-populated, and ill-developed countries, with a view to tempting capital to undertake works of public improvement, are no doubt more or less of the character of monopolies. But as a general rule, monopolies are held in high disfavour in all countries alike, as being inimical to the ultimate welfare of the community as a whole.

The ordinary course of trade, as now generally carried on, is the very antithesis of monopoly. The universal rule is free and unrestrained competition, qualified only by the influence of tariff duties in protecting to certain countries the supply, in a more or less complete degree, of their own requirements.

* "Middle Ages," chap. ix. part ii.   † *Ib.*, vol. ii. p. 385.

Necessarily, in certain cases where new industries are established, those who first engage in them have for a time something like a monopoly of the business. But as a set-off to this often doubtful gain, they have to find new markets for their products, as, for example, in the case of the aluminium industry, which was founded in this country a few years since by my friend, Mr Castner, on a modified process of his own, or in the case of the sodium industry, similarly founded. In these cases, the adventurers run the risk of failing to secure consumers of their products, and if they should be particularly successful in this endeavour, their monopoly soon disappears.

Monopolies are often carried on, and attempted to be carried on by States, as well as by individuals. More than one European State makes the manufacture of tobacco a Government monopoly, and thereby not only increases the price of that commodity to the general consumer, but also, as a rule, limits the range of choice, and furnishes an inferior article. In 1886 Prince Bismarck attempted to secure the consent of the German Reichstag to a proposal to make the manufacture of brandy a Government monopoly. He proposed to buy up at fixed prices all the raw spirits manufactured in the realm, and, after refining them, retail them at home, and export them to foreign countries. The idea underlying the proposal was that the State would thereby be enabled to regulate production, to grant or withhold licenses at pleasure, and to fix prices. The agricultural interest, on the other hand, proposed that the existing manufacturers should form a large association of distillers, the Government to forbid by law the creation of new distilleries; that the Government should pay them about 40 per cent. above the market price for what they produced, to be gathered together in large tanks or magazines, and that from this price the existing tax on spirits, less 10 per cent., should be deducted, and an excise duty of 9½d. a litre be collected on the brandy delivered for home consumption. Neither proposal was adopted, but both are worth putting on record, as instances of how both the State and the individual seek to prey on the community. This principle will be found to underlie and to pervade all the various plans and projects that have been either proposed or carried into effect under the guise of syndicated trade.

One of the most serious indictments brought against the modern syndicate or trust is that it is a monopoly, and as such ought to be restrained by law. But there are different varieties of the *genus* trust or combination, and they are not all designed to establish monopolies, nor have they always that effect, although it is indisputable that many, if not most, of them have that tendency.

The Committee of the House of Representatives which inquired into the working of trusts in the United States in 1888, concluded their report with the opinion that "while the trust may be dangerous, and should be watched over by law, it did not necessarily imply monopoly; that combination has greater power of good and evil than individuals, but that its power for the latter is lessened by the discoveries of the age." The Committee held that "the severest penalties should be prescribed and enforced for every attempt at combination, the object of which may be monopoly or the enhancing of prices."

While the syndicates or trusts that have been established in our own and other countries have not necessarily been monopolies, it is obvious that their objects were likely to be the more successful according as they got the whole or only a part of the business syndicated into their own hands, and if the whole of the business in question was under their control, the organisation became a virtual monopoly in the country of its origin, subject, of course, to whatever influence in the direction of breaking it up might be exercised by imports from other countries.

Thus, in the case of the Standard Oil Trust, in the United States, upwards of 75 per cent. of the total production of refined oil was under control.

In the case of the Sugar Trust, 86 per cent. of all the sugar-refining capacity of the Atlantic Coast was under control, including all the sugar refineries in the State of New York.   As sugar is an article of universal and every-day use, clearly this amount of control involved a large degree of monopoly, the fruits of which were witnessed in a great advance of the price of sugar subsequent to the formation of the trust.   On this point the report made on Trusts by the New York Senate significantly remarked that " no satisfactory explanation has been given of the cause of such advance, apart from the probability that the combination is able to put up prices at its pleasure."

It is argued by the apologists for combinations like the Standard Oil Trust that combinations of capital and of persons, without any grant of exclusive privileges, are in no sense of the word monopolies.

In this argument the word monopoly is narrowed down to its most ancient and restrictive meaning.   It is perfectly true that in former days a monopoly was understood to be a grant by the Government for the sole buying, working, making, or using of anything.   But in these days, the combination of individuals has the power to effect much more in the way of monopoly, if certain conditions are fulfilled, than any evil that was ever done by Government interference, because the area of operations has become so greatly enlarged. Not only so, but it is obvious that such organised monopolies, where successful, are much more subversive of general wellbeing than the monopolies which have been, and still are, due to Government interference. The monopolies granted to railway companies in this country are subject to the right of control by the State of all rates, fares, and other matters of concern. Hardly any monopoly is now established by State aid that is not similarly under control, with a view to safeguarding public interests. But where a monopoly is created by individuals in the manufacture or sale of a commodity, no such control exists, so that the monopolists are left at liberty to make whatever terms they choose with the user or consumer. This being so, it is conceivable that combinations of capital might be organised to control all the principal necessaries of life, and that they might impose such a scale of charges upon the consumers of such commodities as would make it quite impossible for poor people to procure subsistence. Happily this state of things could hardly happen with wheat and some other commodities that are grown universally ; but the tendency is apparent all the same.

It is, however, necessary to discriminate between the combination that results in monopoly and the combination that is engaged in legitimate trade, although the dividing line between them may be as fine as a gossamer web. Combinations must not be condemned, simply because they exist as such. Corporations are often valuable and useful factors in the commonwealth, and undertake enterprises requiring large capital that could not well be carried out without them.

CHAPTER III.

LOW PRICES AND OVER-PRODUCTION.

MOST of the attempts that have been made to control prices have arisen out of the serious depression of business, and the impossibility of securing remunerative rates by natural operations. Similarly, most of the attempts made to limit production have had their origin in the inevitable tendency of competition to induce production on the largest possible scale, which is found, as a rule, to be the cheapest method. What, then, are the remedies available for low prices and over-production? This is a subject that has often been anxiously and earnestly debated, but it has more frequently than not ended in academic discussion. Combinations have been the only really practical attempts made to translate such discussion into effectual action.

Manifestly, if there were no such thing as over-production —in other words, if the supply of a commodity were always a little behind the demand—there would be no such thing as unremunerative prices, for there would be a competition for supplies that would be certain, in the natural order of things, to make prices at least remunerative, and perhaps extremely profitable.

On the 22nd of January 1889, I wrote in *The Times* as follows on this subject, as affecting industrial or manufacturing combinations :—" The industrial syndicate, in its most popular form, and its generally declared aims and objects, is really a protest against, and a remedy for, over-production. The recent advances of science, and especially of applied science, in the concrete instances of textile, ironmaking, and other machinery, have multiplied the means of production far beyond the actual requirements of consumers. In a considerable number of our leading industries there is sufficient productive power available to provide for a very large increase on the shortest possible notice, which means that there is constantly unemployed a considerable amount of invested capital. This is a standing menace to industry, and an irremovable check to the improvement of trade. Let prices advance by ever so little, and production is at once developed so as to keep them down. This, on the whole, is good for consumers, because it guarantees that prices shall be kept moderately low, whereas, if the means of production were equal to the needs of consumers, and no more, prices would be subject to constant and violent fluctuations. It is not, however, satisfactory to manufacturers, and it has tended to keep profits abnormally low for a number of years past. In these circumstances the formation of a syndicate of manufacturers, each of whom is pledged to produce only a certain quantity, and to sell at a specified regulation price, answers just the same purpose as if the productive resources of the trade or industry, in so far as they were in excess of consumption, had been got rid of. In Germany there is a school of economists, headed by M. Kleinwächter, of Innsbrück, which even goes the length of maintaining that the State should form and regulate such syndicates, and should prohibit the erection of works in excess of the wants of the community.

" Syndicated trade is neither more nor less than a revival or modification, under a new set of conditions, of the system

of protection. It is as much an infraction of the principles
of free trade as the Customs tariffs of the United States or
of the German Zollverein. In more than one respect,
indeed, there is a strong family likeness between the two.
A Customs tariff gives to the producers whom it protects the
opportunity of charging higher prices than they would otherwise be able to command within the limits of the duties
which it imposes. The prices fixed by a syndicate are
similarly governed by the conditions of international competition, and must not be fixed so high as to give foreign
rivals the chance of slipping in and occupying the home
market. But a syndicated trade in a country with a protective Customs tariff is necessarily a different thing from a
trade with regulation prices in a country like our own. In
Great Britain the cases are comparatively few in which
syndicates can do much for manufacturers in the way of
raising prices, because our home markets are not protected
by tariff, and a considerable advance of prices would be
likely to admit the foreigner. In protected countries, like
Germany and the United States, syndicates practically put
an end to competition between home producers, and enable
them to reap the full benefit of the higher prices in their
own markets which the tariff secures against outside rivals
and competitors. It is because there has, within recent
years, been such an increase of productive resources in high-
tariff countries as to lead to the same kind of free-fighting
trade among home manufacturers as would occur in the
absence of a tariff, that syndicates have become so
numerous."

There is, however, a remarkable periodicity about the
occurrence of acute industrial depression, and while at one
time low prices are the rule, they become at other times

the exception. Every now and again production is over-taken by consumption, and thereupon there is a great rise ; but this does not last for long, because every one is in a hurry to take advantage of the higher range of prices, until comparative scarcity is resolved into an absolute glut. There-upon depression again becomes the order of the day, and an era of unprofitable business is once more ushered in.

In a valuable study of this subject, issued some years ago by the United States Government,* industrial depression is attributed " First, to competition, or the attempts among manufacturers to undersell each other, by which they re-duced wages to a low average ; second, to the state of the currency and banking system, which afforded at one time undue facilities to over-trading, and again caused fatal re-vulsions in trade ; third, to the corn laws, as keeping up the price of bread by the exclusion of foreign corn, thus giving a monopoly to landowners, and forcing the foreign capi-talist to resort to manufactures instead of agriculture ; and enabling foreign manufacturers, from the cheapness of food abroad, and its dearness in Great Britain, to undersell the British manufacturer—results leading to the transfer of the cotton manufacture to America and to the Continent of Europe ; and, fourth, to the faulty methods of manufac-ture." These earlier influences were, in later years, aided and abetted by another, which was probably more potent than them all—the over-production of commodities, due to the introduction of improved machinery in all staple manu-factures. With all the advantages that it confers in the way of improved and more economical production, machin-ery has brought about a very large displacement of labour,

* " Industrial Depressions : First Annual Report of the United States Commissioner of Labour," p. 17.

which, so far as the labour displaced is concerned, tends to cripple the purchasing power of the community.

Over-production would not of itself be necessarily a bad thing for the producers, were it not associated with competition; and with competition, as a rule, of a very anxious and fiercely-contested description. This competition immediately results in the cutting of prices, so that, in the struggle for orders, and in order to retain old customers, rates are quoted that are often far from remunerative.

The function and aim of the modern syndicate or trust is to get rid of this competition over as large an area as possible, by limiting production, and making a common interest among producers. The end in view is not necessarily to advance prices. In the case of two of the most notable trusts on record—the Standard Oil and the Cottonseed Oil trusts in the United States—prices were not advanced, but, on the contrary, fell considerably. In both cases, however, the profits made were largely increased—due partly to the concentration of management and unity of action, and partly to improvements introduced into production and distribution. It may, therefore, be held that, if prices are not necessarily reduced, profits must be increased, or the object of the combination would not be realised.

It is generally admitted that over-production is a great evil. If it were possible to remedy that evil effectually, without injury or mischief to other interests, a valuable end would be achieved. Hitherto, however, the only really effective method adopted for gaining that end has been the formation of a syndicate or combination of producers to regulate the output.

"What, after all," says Bastiat, "is competition? Is it a thing existing and acting by itself, like the cholera? No.

It is evident that competition is liberty. To destroy liberty
of action is to destroy the possibility, and, therefore, the
faculty of choosing, judging, comparing—to destroy intelligence, thought, man himself. From whatever point they
start, modern reformers always end here. To ameliorate
society, they begin by annihilating the individual. . . .
Rightly considered, every man in this world is responsible
for providing for his own satisfaction by his own efforts."

Everything that Bastiat here contends for as desirable
and valuable is necessarily more or less sacrificed by the
only available remedy for over-production, except annihila-
tion or bankruptcy. The cure is likely to be regarded by
many, for that reason, as a good deal worse than the
disease.

One of the most obvious disadvantages incidental to the
establishment of a union or trust for the regulation of production, or of prices, or both, is the almost inevitable
stimulus that it gives to the increase of foreign competition,
as well as of the means of production at home. As one
example among many of how this influence operates to the
detriment of the export trade of a country, the case of the
English Bleaching Powder Association may be cited. This
organisation was founded about the year 1884, and for six
years kept down the quantity and kept up·the price. During
its existence the commodity under regulation was advanced
so much in price that Continental countries were induced
to largely extend their means of production. In the case
of France, which had formerly been a good customer of
British manufactures, the means of production were so largely
augmented, that the home output became practically sufficient for the wants of the country, and England lost a valued
and important customer.

Not only so, but the raising of the cost of a commodity that is in every-day use has a tendency to cause customers to seek other sources of supply. When the question of forming a chemical union was under discussion in the autumn of 1890, it was pointed out that the mere prospect of the formation of such a syndicate had caused the price of caustic soda to advance by 25 per cent. or 30 per cent. above its former level, and that consequently orders which formerly came to English firms from the Baltic, the Black Sea, and other markets, were going to Germany, while German makers were also likely to compete for the English home trade, which was one of great value.

There must, of course, be limits, either natural or artificial, to the extent to which foreign countries can wrest orders under such conditions. Where a commodity it produced in a country under peculiarly favourable circumstances, as is the case with the iron ores of Cleveland, or the coke supplies of South Durham, it is possible that a regulated price may not help foreign nations, as against our own, provided that the regulated price is not too high. But this is not a general rule. In the great majority of cases, there is only a very narrow margin between the price at which English manufacturers can produce a commodity, and the price at which it can be produced abroad, so that a comparatively small rise of price will afford to the foreign manufacturers the coveted opportunity of acquiring a new market. In all such cases, the temporary gain of an artificially better price usually brings its Nemesis in the form of an ultimate disorganisation and loss of business.

Mr S. C. T. Dodd, the solicitor to the Standard Oil Company, has made the following forcible remarks on agreements to prevent competition and fixing prices and production under our present laws :—

"It may still be asserted that it is contrary to common law to enter into arrangements or agreements to prevent or diminish competition, to lessen production, or to enhance prices.

"Made in that form, the proposition can neither be affirmed nor denied. If it is asserted that *each* and *all* agreements of that nature are illegal the statement is absurdly false. Our most ordinary and beneficial business agreements and arrangements have such tendencies and effects. If the assertion is that *some* such agreements and arrangements are illegal the assertion is correct. And right here is the key to the popular misunderstandings relative to what the law is and ought to be on this subject. It is common to assert that the law forbids agreements in restraint of competition and to restrict production and to enhance prices, when the meaning and the truth is the law forbids *some* such agreements. The vice of the proposed laws is that they would prevent *all* such agreements, and thus make illegal the most essential business contracts.

"The line between those that are legal and those that are illegal has never been clearly defined. If legislatures would define such a line they might be legislating to some good purpose. To get rid of the difficulty by invalidating all agreements to enhance prices, &c., is simple insanity. It is like declaring *all* agreements criminal, because *some* agreements are contrary to public policy.

"To render such agreements illegal there must be added an element of improper motive, chicanery or fraud. There must be a purpose to prejudice the public or to oppress individuals by extortion or mischief. Or the combination or arrangement must be of such a character as to prevent *general* competition, and to control prices to such an extent as to constitute a legal monopoly.

"This is quite different from the proposition that *all* arrangements and agreements having the tendency to diminish competition or affect production and prices are illegal. 'A party may legally purchase the trade and business of another for the very purpose of preventing competition.' (Diamond Match Co. *v.* Roeber, 106 N. Y., 473.) 'Excessive competition may sometimes result in actual injury to the public, and anti-competitive contracts to avert personal ruin may be perfectly reasonable.' (Horner *v.* Graves, 7 Bing., 735.) 'Honest co-operation, though it might prevent the rivalry of parties, and thus lessen competition, is not forbidden by public policy.' (Atcheson *v.* Mallin, 43 N. Y., 147.) Chief Justice Shaw, in Com. *v.* Hunt, 4 Metcalf, 134, supposes the case of a number of persons, believing the price of bread too high, proposing to the village baker that if he did not reduce his prices they would set up a rival establishment and sell bread at lower prices. 'It might be said and proved,' says the Chief Justice, ' that the purpose of the associates was to diminish his profits, and thus to impoverish him, though the ultimate and laudable object of the combination was to reduce the cost of bread to themselves and their neighbours. The same thing may be said of all competition in every branch of trade and industry ; and yet it is through that competition that the best interests in trade and industry are promoted. We think, therefore, that associations may be entered into the object of which is to adopt measures that may have a tendency to impoverish another, and yet, so far from being criminal or unlawful, the object may be highly meritorious and public spirited.'

"The law as it is corresponds with good business sense. Under the law as it is proposed to be, such an association would be criminal, inasmuch as it is an agreement, arrangement, and combination to fix, regulate, and reduce prices, and tending to force another out of business.

"We might further suppose that the aforesaid baker, finding ruin inevitable as a competitor, proposed to join the association. Under the law as it is, this would be as legal as it is sensible. Under the laws proposed, it would be criminal, because it would be an agreement, arrangement, and combination having the effect and tendency to diminish competition.

"Suppose, further, that the price of flour should rise, or that working men should demand higher wages, and this association, finding that it also must be ruined if it sold bread at the same price, agreed to advance prices to correspond with the increased cost of material and manufacture, its object still being, however, to sell at the lowest profitable figure. Such action, under the law as it is, would be justifiable, and any other course would be blind idiocy. Under the proposed law it would be criminal, being an agreement to enhance prices.

"Suppose, further, that prices being thus increased, consumption was lessened, and the association agreed to lessen their production of bread accordingly. This, under the law as it is, is an every-day occurrence in every man's business. Under the law as it is proposed to be, it would be criminal, because it is an agreement to lessen production. And if afterwards consumption should increase, and the association should agree to enlarge their bakery, and do a larger business than before, they would again be criminals in agreeing to fix, regulate, and limit production.

"In Marsh *v.* Russell, 66 N. Y., 292, the Court says: 'When business is carried on by a firm its members could regulate the price at which they would buy and sell. Suppose they had formed a partnership to buy and sell wheat, how can it be doubted that they could lawfully agree in their articles of copartnership that neither member of the firm should come in competition with the firm, and that wheat should not be purchased for more than a certain price, nor sold for less than a certain price? Such an agreement would certainly not upon its face be unlawful.' It is different, however, says the Court, when 'there could be no apparent purpose for such an agreement except to prevent competition between the parties thereto.'

"In Phippen *v.* Stickney, 2 Metcalf, 384, the rule is laid down that agreements to prevent competition are valid when they evince an honest purpose of carrying out a legitimate enterprise, but otherwise when the circumstances evince a fraudulent purpose. And Chief Justice Coleridge, in the late case of the Mogul S. S. Co., says 'the line between legal and illegal acts affecting competition is difficult to draw, that if the acts are done wrongly or maliciously, or in furtherance of a wrongful and malicious combination, they are actionable. Trade not being infinite, what one man gains another loses. But persons have a right to push their trade by all lawful means. Amongst lawful means is certainly included the inducing, by profitable offers, customers to deal with them rather than with their rivals.'"

A very interesting article on the subject of trusts, contributed by Professor Jenks to the *Economic Journal* for

March 1892, describes the statistical history of trusts in the
United States, and points out that, whatever their avowed
purpose may be, and although sometimes the trust may
exist coincidently with a tolerably low range of prices, the
general tendency of the system is to increase the cost of
commodities to the consumers.   The Sugar Trust, the
Whisky Trust, and other trusts are quoted as notable
examples of this tendency.

CHAPTER IV.

THE FUNCTION OF THE STATE.

MUCH has been written on the part that the Government of a State should play in reference to combinations designed to limit production, to augment prices artificially, to create a scarcity of a necessary commodity, or to injure by any similar means the interests of consumers, as such. The tendency of all such movements is to create monopolies of the worst kind, and in another chapter I have dealt with the subject from the monopoly point of view. But there are those who would go much farther than imposing pains and penalties against the worst evils of monopolies. The fact that monopolies tend to create scarcity and increase prices has always been cited against them, and used for their suppression, so that monopolists have had a hard fight to maintain their existence. But there are obvious reasons why legislation, intended to keep down monopoly, should stop short of any interference with legitimate enterprise, and should not make it entirely impossible to adopt what may be perfectly proper and much-needed expedients to cure the manifold evils of over-production and cut-throat competition.

The economic history of England up to about a hundred years ago is almost one continuous record of statutory interference with the natural course of prices, either by granting monopolies, or by fixing by an arbitrary procedure the prices

at which labour as well as commodities should be sold.
Nowadays these sumptuary laws are universally reprobated,
and modern nations have passed over from the extremist
forms of paternal government to a *régime* under which the
liberty of the subject is paramount, and the prevailing creed
is that the greatest service that the State can render to
commerce and industry is to let them alone. The public
are supposed to be strong enough, in matters of commerce
at any rate, to look after themselves, and in a general way
this view of the case is tolerably correct. The position
which some German economists have taken up is, however,
quite opposed to the theory just stated. It is even argued
that the Government should interfere to prevent the multi-
plication of the means of production beyond a certain fixed
limit, and that the State should fix the *minimum* rate of
profit that capital should earn. The sturdy, self-reliant
Englishman will certainly not adopt this view. The operation on an extensive scale of a system of rings or monopolies, designed to increase artificially the cost of production, or to limit the quantity of any commodity that is
available at a particular time, or in these or other ways to
advance the price to the consumer and increase the profit
of the producer, is, at the best, an anachronism in a country
that is professedly wedded to the principles of free trade.
For the effect of a successful combination of this kind is
exactly similar to that which would be produced by the
adoption of a national system of protection of industry, so
far, at least, as the consumer is concerned. The main
difference is that, under a national system of protection,
such as that which we see operating in the United States,
all important industries are alike participants in the supposed benefits resulting from the exclusion of foreign pro-

duce, whereas, in the case of the syndicated industry, the benefits, if any, do not travel beyond itself. Protection, as a general system, has, moreover, this much in its favour, that it allows labour, as well as capital, to share in its fruits, whereas, in the case of a syndicated industry, the capitalists do not consider that any one outside their own immediate circle is entitled to participate in their gains. There are, of course, imaginable, and perhaps, in some cases, even actual limits within which the operations of a system of pools or monopolies of this kind would become intolerable. It is conceivable, although in the highest degree unlikely, that a pool of capitalists might buy up all the existing supplies of wheat, or potatoes, or other produce that is in every-day demand, and render its acquisition by the general public extremely difficult, and by a large section of the poorer classes all but impossible. But even when a syndicate has obtained full possession of all the available supplies of a commodity—or, in other words, has " cornered " the market—there are always at work, in a greater or less degree, influences which determine the possible limits within which prices can be successfully raised. Those are : —

1. The competition of foreign countries.

2. The purchasing power of the general public.

3. The facilities and inducements presented to home competition.

The first of these causes has already been referred to. It is always at work with regard to the great majority of industrial or commercial operations. Whether it is in food supplies, in minerals, in textiles, or in general manufactures, there is always, in a free-trade country, a liability to have the objects of a trading syndicate defeated by the competition of foreign countries, if prices are artificially raised to a point that deprives the industry in question of the extent of advantage that it usually enjoys from its local circumstances. In the case of a protectionist country this advantage is invariably *plus* the extent of the protection, and *plus* also the cost of transport from the country that would be most likely to compete. In a free-trade country the artificially-created price must be kept much lower than in a country where prices are fixed by tariff provisions, and hence the United States could, in the great majority of cases, fix a much higher range of prices, under a pooling arrangement, than we in Great Britain could do, without being affected by the determinant of outside competition. Even, however, in a country like the United States, natural laws have always interposed to prevent artificially-created prices from being maintained for any great length of time. The area of the country, and the variety of its resources, are such that, even if outside competition were of no account as a regulator of prices, the internal competition of one district or State with another would always compel a moderately low range of prices. The United States have adopted more gigantic, and perhaps, on the whole, more successful industrial combinations than any other country in the world. We are told, indeed, that "every branch of hardware, from rails to carpet tacks, has its combination to keep up prices or restrict production. The cases are only too frequent where the combination pays certain mills for not running more than they could earn by running. For lumber and for paper, for cattle and for milk, for cartridges and for matches, in each business there is an organised combination, fixing rates and often limiting production. The waterways themselves, which, we are so often told, are to protect

us from the monopoly of the railroad, have their rates fixed
and their traffic pooled by combinations of greater or less
influence, from the local barge association of some interior
town to the great North Atlantic Steam Conference." *
And yet the cases in which proved abuses have occurred in
connection with this vast system of pooling and monopoly
have been remarkably few. The Anthracite Coal Combination, which was carried on for a number of years, was
denounced by the Governor of the State of Pennsylvania as
"a pool which has for long periods kept the mines running
on three-quarter time, thus putting nearly 100,000 workers
on what amounted to three-quarter pay," and as having,
"by hindering competition, restricted the development of
our great mineral wealth." For these reasons, it was proposed that the combination should be broken up by legislative enactment, but hitherto the force of public opinion
has not been strong enough to bring about this result. As
a matter of fact, the combination has not raised prices to
such a point as to be a source of real grievance to consumers, and in spite of the existence of this powerful pool,
the prices of both coal and coke in the United States are
generally lower than in any other country.† It is the same
with many other so-called trusts or pools. The Cotton-
seed Oil Trust, the Fertilizer's Combination, the Western
Whisky Pool, the Indiarubber Trust, the Sugar Trust, the
Standard Oil Company, and many "others of that ilk"

* Hadley's "Railroad Transportation," p. 68.

† Enormous quantities of small coal have been sold in the United
States at less than 2s. 6d. per ton ; and coke for iron-making purposes
has been sold over long periods at less than 5s. per ton. The average
cost of the bituminous coal produced in the United States, as a whole,
in 1889, was under 4s., and in many cases it did not exceed 3s.

have all been organised on a basis which, while it secures centralisation and economy of working, and often makes large demands upon the railway companies for low rates of transport, is yet without appreciable detriment to the public at large.

So far as the public interest is concerned in or affected by so-called "trusts" or combinations of either producers or sellers, I wrote in *The Times* in 1889 as follows :—

"The success that has attended the application of this system has been so marked, and in some cases so phenomenal, that there is a great temptation to carry it further, in the absence of any restraining influence. We may, indeed, if present appearances are not greatly deceptive, live to see the food that we eat, the clothes that we wear, the railways upon which we travel, the ships in which we sail, and the labour which we purchase controlled by organisations of the kind named. The only element that is wanting in order to make the operation of the system of syndicated trade universal is that of loyal consent on the part of every individual who would be likely to come into competition with the parties to any particular combination. There is no reason why a combination of three or four manufacturers should be more successful than one of three or four thousand, except that the proportions of the smaller body are more manageable, and the loyalty which is indispensable to the maintenance of such a compact is thereby more likely to be assured. The experience of syndicates or combinations has, however, proved that, even over a wide area, embracing many leading producers and industries, combination may be resorted to in such a way as to crush out competition. The case of the Standard Oil Company in America, already referred to, is a case in point. It is now more than

twenty-two years since a small syndicate in the United
States got hold of a new process for refining petroleum,
which gave them an advantage over their competitors. The
company did not, in this case, attain to its ultimate monopoly by inviting rival concerns to join it, in order that competition might be extinguished, but it compelled its rivals
to join its ranks or to withdraw from the field by selling at
prices with which they could not compete. This process,
which was really that of the survival of the fittest up to a
certain point, ultimately gave the Standard Oil Company
the control of nearly all the refineries in the United States,
whereupon they were able to dictate the prices that should
be charged in each district, and throttled all independent
competition. It has never, however, been alleged that the
public, as such, has suffered by this particular case. On
the contrary, prices have declined rather than advanced, the
quality of the oil has been improved, and it is even doubtful
whether the public would have been equally well served
under a system of free competition. But there have been
notable examples of a different character. The copper ring
ran up the price of copper to double what it had been under
a system of free competition. The cost of tin was in a
similar manner advanced, at a bound, to an almost prohibi-
tory price. What, therefore, is wanted, in order to relieve
the public mind from the disquietude that is produced by
operations of this kind, is a guarantee that, while the rights
of the individual shall not be unduly restrained, those of the
community shall be respected and preserved. It may be
doubted whether it is a right of the community that it shall
be protected from the rapacity of pools, rings, or corners
that operate in a legitimate way. This, however, may be
taken for granted under certain conceivable circumstances,

as, for example, the 'cornering' of wheat or other necessaries of life, so as to make it impossible for all but the rich
to purchase supplies.   The rest is only a question of
degree."

Following up these remarks, I cannot do better than reproduce the following observations that I made on the
function of the State in reference to this subject :—

" In considering how far the interposition of the State is
called for, we must not forget, first of all, to distinguish
between the rings that are carried on for the legitimate
purposes of trade—that is, primarily, to secure a reasonable
profit for the producers—and the rings that are contrived for
the purpose of buying up all the existing supply of a commodity, and thereupon demanding prices that are out of all
relation to the cost of the product.   The first is legitimate
business ; the second is speculation pure and simple.   The
industrial combination which seeks to temporarily alleviate
the evils of over-production by pooling the business at prices
that leave only a fair profit to the producers pursues methods
which are, indeed, open to exception, and perhaps even to
grave condemnation, but often as the lesser of two notorious
evils, and only with the object of obtaining that to which its
members are entitled, but which they cannot otherwise
command—a reasonable profit in the pursuit of their trade.
The commercial syndicate is usually without a conscience
or a legitimate aim, and seeks only to ' fleece ' the public to
the utmost extent of its power.

" While, therefore, there is a wide difference in character,
in methods, and in aims, between these two typical forms of
the modern trade combination, both are alike amenable to
the laws that prohibit any association of individuals for the
purpose of raising prices.   In the United Kingdom this

offence was formerly dealt with, under the old statutes re-
lating to forestalling and regrating, in the severest possible
way. The conspiracy laws still in operation are probably sufficiently comprehensive to bring offenders within their meshes.
In France the Penal Code (Article 419) prohibits any combination for the purpose of raising or lowering prices, under
the penalty of at least one month's imprisonment and a fine
of 500f. to 10,000f. In the United States, Congress was
recently called upon to inquire into the constitution of some
of the existing trusts or pools, with a view to legislation that
would enable them to be controlled, if not entirely prevented. In Germany there is not, in practice at any rate,
any legislative bar to syndicated trade, and syndicates,
therefore, flourish apace. All countries, however, have had,
or are having, the attention of their chief economists and
statesmen directed to the advance of the movement and
the evils which are threatened thereby, so that we shall
probably before long hear more of the matter. How far is
the State likely to go? Will the individual still be permitted to bring into play all the vast power with which unlimited command of capital and skilful organisation can
endow him, in order that he may enrich himself at the
expense of the community by a *coup de main*, or will he be
restrained in the exercise of this power in some limited
degree? And, if restraint is to be imposed, where is the
line to be drawn? Will the State determine what is a fair
rate of profit per ton to the manufacturer of pig-iron or
steel rails, and fix his powers of combination within those
limits? If so, what hypothetical standard can be adopted,
seeing that no two manufacturers are in precisely the same
economic circumstances? Again, how can the State reasonably interfere with the means taken to secure profits for the

manufacturer, seeing that it will not, and, indeed, could not, relieve him of his losses? These considerations suggest a few only of the great cloud of difficulties that would be likely to arise in attempting to legislate on a question of this kind. Bad, therefore, as the alternative of leaving the public at the mercy of such organisations may appear, any legislation that would have the effect of tying the hands of the capitalist, and thereby checking legitimate enterprise, would possibly, in the long run, make matters worse."

In another chapter I have dealt with the special legislation proposed or attempted in the United States with the view of checking the movement for the establishment of large industrial and distributive combinations. One of the most important of these—the Sherman Anti-Trust Act— has not hitherto been mentioned. This measure has been more debated, more praised, and more abused than any other measure of its kind hitherto brought forward in the United States. The avowed object of the act is the laudable one of " protecting trade and commerce against unlawful restraints and monopolies." There was a great deal of hostility and opposition to the act, but it ultimately became law in a modified form, and the Government of the United States at once proceeded to institute prosecutions under its ægis. The Whisky and the Sugar Trusts were two of the first to be brought to book. But the fear of being made the victims of suits for personal damage has apparently slackened the zeal of those who are immediately responsible for carrying out the provisions of the law, and another obstacle that has stood in its way has been the absence of adequate appropriations for meeting the expenditure which the law entails.*

* It is one of the curious phenomena of American jurisprudence that

Action has, however, been taken under the Sherman Act
in a few notable cases—one of them the case of the
Mississippi lumbermen.

The members of the Mississippi Valley Lumbermen's
Association were prosecuted in the Federal Courts recently
under the Sherman Anti-Trust Law, on an indictment
charging them with having made an agreement and conspiring together to advance the price of common pine
lumber to $11.50 per 1000, which was 50 cents more than
the prevailing price. Judge Nelson, sitting in the United
States District Court at St Paul, sustained a demurrer to
the indictment, holding that, in order to show an offence
under the statute, it must be alleged that the accused con-
spired together to advance the price of some commodity,
actually had advanced it, and had a complete monopoly of
the trade in the given article within the affected locality;
that the advance must also be above a just and reasonable
price, and that if the conspiring parties do not have a complete monopoly, the competition of other dealers will compel
the advanced price of an article to go to its proper and
reasonable price. In giving judgment he further said:
" While it may be true that some of the dealers might
attempt to induce purchasers to be governed by the price
fixed in their locality by the parties to the agreement, and
try to keep up prices, yet competition in the commodity
would soon bring the price down unless there were fraudulent
or coercive means resorted to for the purpose of restraining
other dealers, and preventing them from exercising their
own judgment as to prices. An agreement between a

every Government official incurs penalties for expenditure in excess of
specific appropriations, so that a law may be practically inoperative, if
enough money has not been voted to carry out its provisions.

number of dealers and manufacturers to raise prices, unless they practically controlled the entire commodity, cannot operate as a restraint upon trade, nor does it tend to injuriously affect the public. Unless the agreement involves the absorption of the entire traffic in timber, and is entered into for the purpose of obtaining the entire control of it for extortionate objects, it is not objectionable to the statute, in my opinion. Competition is not stifled by such an agreement, and other dealers would soon force the parties to the agreement to sell at the market price, or a reasonable price at least." In this case, therefore, which was one of the first tried under its provisions, the operation of the Anti-Trust Law was not such as its author and promoters intended.

Nevertheless, the Department of Justice has for some time been engaged in collecting evidence against the principal trusts in the United States, and it is understood that more definite action will be taken by and by. A recent announcement was made to the effect that this evidence "lacks legal completeness," and that "several important links are missing to constitute such legal evidence as would enable the Government to succeed in a prosecution. But the matter has by no means been hung up indefinitely. In July 1891, a circular letter was issued by the State Department to all the district attorneys throughout the country, instructing them to "examine this (the Anti-Trust) law carefully with a view to ascertain whether it is being violated within your district," and requiring them, in such a case, to use their best efforts "to indict and prosecute the wrong-doers, as well as to enforce the law by civil proceedings, as provided in the act."

Perhaps the most important case hitherto taken up under the Anti-Trust Law is that known as the Tennessee case.

This case is so important, as bearing on the future of trusts in the United States, that its history may briefly be set down.

The Jellico Mountain Coal and Coke Company was mainly operated in Kentucky, and its output was sold to the Coal Exchange in Nashville, Tennessee, the members of the exchange agreeing to rule the trade, and keep out all non-supporters who mined coal. They fixed the rate of freight handling and percentage, and formed a " combine " without let or hindrance.

Five months after the passage of the Anti-Trust Act, the Government made application for authority from the Circuit Court of Middle Tennessee to seize the coal and restrain the exchange from continuing its business. The court denied the application on the ground that the plaintiff (the United States) showed no disposition to file an indemnifying bond in the event of its being shown that the charge was not sustained on legal inquisition. The court held, in denying the Government's attempt to use its authority in such a way, that harm done to individuals would be serious and real, and they would be without redress from such arrogating proceedings, whereas the Government would not suffer in the cause of justice if it waited until it could proceed in due form.

Next year, in 1891, the Government got possession of the agreement between the members of the exchange and the mines, and this was in evidence, showing conclusively that it was a combination, and plainly in violation of the Anti-Trust Act, passed in July 1890. The defence had nothing to urge in support of its position, save that the act was unconstitutional. The Government gained its suit, and the exchange was required to restrain its operations within the ordinary methods of dealing in coal and coke. "Since then," sententiously remarks a chronicler of the case, "the coal combines have not left their agreements lying around for the United States district attorneys to pick up."

Among other cases that have been taken up under the Anti-Trust Law, mention may be made of the combination of distillers and cattle-feeders in Massachusetts, against the officers of whom indictments were found, the Sugar Trust in the Eastern district of Pa., the Butterine Trust, and several others, while many different cases were "on the file." It appears to be probable, therefore, that before long the American trust will have to fight hard for its existence, and we may even be called upon to chronicle its entire disappearance from the field of industrial operations.

CHAPTER V.

THE LIMITATION OF THE VEND IN THE NORTH OF ENGLAND COAL TRADE.

ONE of the most important, and, on the whole, successful combinations that have ever been established in the United Kingdom for keeping up prices and restricting competition, was that known in the history of the North of England coal trade as "the vend." This combination, which was limited to the counties of Durham and Northumberland, at a time when these counties produced nearly, if not quite, one-half of all the coal raised in the country, was carried on, with occasional, but seldom long-continued, interruptions, for a period of about seventy years.

The "vend" was established in the year 1771, for the purpose of securing for the coal-owners in the two counties already named, the advantage of a permanently and uniformly higher price, and the chief means adopted to this end was to restrict the production at a time when coal was coming into much greater demand. Matthias Dunn states that "after 1773, the influx of collieries produced such an over-supply that regulation was imperatively called for." *

This organisation had the effect of greatly increasing the cost, not of coal only, but of many other commodities. Within ten years the wages of miners had increased some 50 per cent. Iron, leather, ropes, timber, and powder were

* "View of the Coal Trade of the North of England."

all largely advanced in price. The Parliamentary Committee of 1800 reported that the increased cost of working
coal between 1792 and 1800 was not less than 9s. 10d. per
Newcastle chaldron (thirty-six Winchester bushels), including leading charges, materials, and other items of outlay, as
well as labour. The coal-owners were accustomed to meet
each year, and fix what was called the basis of the vend—
that was, "an assumed quantity to establish the scale of
proportion" between the Tyne and the Wear. The basis
was a purely arbitrary one, and in practice it was often
exceeded. Meanwhile, however, prices were kept up to a
point that had previously been all but unknown. The
Parliamentary Committee of 1800, after taking a great deal
of evidence relative to the conditions under which the combination of coal-owners in the north was carried on, recommended that stringent measures should be taken to put
down the organisation, and to encourage the use of inland
coal. Sixteen years previously an Act of Parliament was
passed against unlawful combinations to advance the price
of coal. This Act provided that any number of persons
above five buying and re-selling coal should be punished by
indictment. The northern combination, however, was not
thereby annulled. It continued in existence until other
circumstances, inherent to the trade itself, brought about its
dissolution. The trade had, in point of fact, become too
large and too widespread to be easily manageable. When
the coal combination was constituted in 1771, the coal
trade of the United Kingdom was almost entirely limited
to the great northern coalfield. The sea-sale, or export,
collieries, were in very few hands. So lately as 1810 there
were only thirty-four such collieries in the North of England,
producing a total quantity of 1,333,000 chaldrons. In

the same year there were thirty-five land-sale, or inland, collieries, which produced only 147,000 chaldrons. It was a comparatively easy matter to regulate so small a trade, while other districts were as yet too much in embryo to offer serious rivalry.

In the ante-railway period, when the great northern coal-field, by virtue of its prestige, its rare natural resources, and its contiguity to the sea-board, could almost command a monopoly of the export trade, both foreign and coast-wise, there was little difficulty found in the working of this combination, which aimed at keeping up prices by limiting supply. But when the growth of the railway system enabled other coal-fields to come to the front, and even to rival Durham and Northumberland in markets that had previously been the almost exclusive monopoly of these counties, the difficulty of maintaining a protective tariff of prices became insuperable. There were, besides, dissensions and disloyalty within the camp. Inequalities in the "basis," or quantity of coal allowed to be vended by each colliery, were complained of. The committee who managed the affairs of the "vend" were alleged to be remiss in enforcing the regulations provided for the punishment of those who did not strictly adhere to the terms of the combination. A number of coal-owners were found to have lowered the price of their coals, to induce more trade, contrary to the arrangements of the committee. But the main and immediate cause of the "vend" being broken up was the unprecedented accumulation of "overs" and "shorts," the former being the quantities produced in excess of the vend allowed by the committee, and the latter the quantities under the regulation allowance. It was found, when stock was taken in May 1845, that the "overs" were as follows:—

	Tons.
The Tyne, with Hartley and Blyth, .	108,680
The Wear, ...	76,056
The Tees, ...	15,227
Total, ...	199,163

The "shorts" at the same time were as follows :—

	Tons.
The Tyne, including Hartley and Blyth,	216,837
The Wear, ...	163,946
The Tees, ...	95,190
Total, ...	475,973

In 1844-5, there was a great strike of pitmen in the North, and to this fact was attributed the very diversified and unequal state of the "shorts" and "overs," which rendered futile the endeavours of the committee to apportion the supply to the demand, and thus secure remunerative prices, without which the continuance of the regulation ceased to be either advantageous or desirable. Under the regulation "vend" it was found that the amount due as penalties in respect of the above overs was not less than £49,790, which the committee proposed to reduce to £29,874, and the latter amount they proposed to pay over to those having "shorts," the aggregate of which was considerably more than double the amount of the "overs." It may be added, as an instance of the want of discipline and loyalty that preceded the complete dissolution of the vend, that upwards of £10,000 was claimed from three coal-owners in respect of their "overs," or excess of the quantity allowed to be vended. At a meeting of the coal

trade, held at Newcastle on the 13th May 1845, the regula-
lation was formally declared at an end, and steps were
taken to wind it up.

It was only to be expected that when each coal-owner
found himself at liberty to produce as much coal as he
pleased, and to sell at such prices and in such markets as
suited his own inclination or convenience, there should at
once arise a desperate struggle for a first place. A free
fighting trade was established throughout the whole of the
northern coal-field, and the coal-owners engaged in the unprofitable game of "beggar my neighbour." About this
time the late Mr Joseph Pease stated in Parliament that he
had given away over 10,000 tons of coal to mend the roads
with, the price obtained in the London and other markets
being so low that they would not pay the cost of freight.
Other coal-owners bore similar testimony.

Various expedients were proposed with a view to affording relief to the trade. It was recommended that the
system which then prevailed of selling coals to buyers in the
North should be abandoned, and that all coals should be
sent direct to London, and sold, so as to avoid the loss
suffered by the coal passing through two markets, experience
having shown that this system had an inevitable tendency
to reduce the higher market to the level of the lower. A
scheme was also launched for the construction of a coal
railway between Newcastle and London. It was promised
in the prospectus of this undertaking, that it would enable
the North country coal-owners to supply the metropolis with
coal 20 per cent. cheaper than it was supplied by sea, while
it was anticipated that, by the entire exclusion of passenger
traffic, the risk of accident would be greatly diminished.
It was, moreover, declared that the experiences of the

London and Birmingham Railway proved that coal might be brought the entire distance from the northern collieries to London at one-half the cost of conveyance by ships, and still leave a profit of 10 per cent. upon a capital of £5,000,000 sterling!

But every scheme, expedient, and remedy projected or attempted with the view of bolstering up the coal trade in the dark days of 1846-47 paled its ineffectual fires before the proposal to confederate all the coal-owners and collieries in the North under one company and under one management. This concern was to bear the name of the London, Durham, and Northumberland Coal Company. Its prospectus, privately printed, is now before us, and bears date February 10th, 1847. It was estimated that the aggregate capital of the Company would be about sixteen millions sterling, but no money was to be required from the shareholders, who, on assigning their respective collieries over to the Company, were at once to receive the amount at which they had previously been valued in the shares of the Company. As a reason for the carrying out of such an unusual project, it was stated that for the two previous years the coal trade had been in a very depressed state, the coal-owners had been suffering loss instead of profit, and each was participating in the general ruin which he fondly hoped would fall only on his neighbour, so that while the consumer derived little benefit from the depreciation, he paid dearly for it when the natural and inevitable reaction took place. In the meantime, the intermediate class made a profit of every fluctuation which it became its interest to promote. "If," it was added, "this ruinous system continue much longer, many collieries will be closed, and those which survive would seek to make up their losses by charging exorbitant prices for the limited quantity they would supply to the public." It was, however, anticipated that "these high prices would speedily induce competition, which would reduce them again to a losing level, and the coal-owner would suffer even greater loss than that previously experienced." It can hardly be necessary to add that, although the scheme promised that the coal-owners would "at once derive a profit, instead of any longer incurring the loss under which they have recently suffered," and although it offered the advantage of a steady range of prices, "while the owners, by receiving a fair remuneration for their capital, skill, and labour, would be enabled to continue their operations, and provide a regular and ample supply," it came to grief almost before it had fairly taken shape, and it will only be remembered in the time to come as a flagrant violation of the first principles of political economy, and a failure as gigantic as the project out of which it arose.

Numerous other expedients were suggested during the year 1847, and in succeeding years, to keep up the prices of coals, and one arrangement after another was made among the coal-owners for that purpose, but all of them ultimately fell through from their want of adaptation to the circumstances of the trade. The coal mining industry of the North of England had become too gigantic a thing, and was allied to too many other interests, to render possible any successful attempt to protect it or make it a monopoly. And if it was impossible then, it has surely become much more so now, when the trade has almost trebled in extent and importance, and has to confront a keen and watchful rival on every side. But while the coal trade has altered in this respect, it has undergone a change in another direction which it is much more pleasing to pursue, and from which much more hopeful auguries are expected.

The depression of 1844-47 led to serious disputes, terminating in a lengthened suspension of labour between employers and employed. The strike of 1844 is one that will live in the annals of the trade long after the generation that witnessed it has been gathered to its fathers ; it commenced on the 5th of April 1844, and laid idle for a period of eighteen weeks almost every colliery in Durham and Northumberland. The men resumed work after enduring much misery and privation, and although they did not succeed in securing an immediate redress of the grievances which induced the struggle, their efforts bore ultimate fruit in the awakening of public sympathy on their behalf, and the redress of their worst grievances by Parliament. The present generation has improved upon all this. The state of the miners generally, and of the Northern miners in particular, is very different to-day to what it was in 1844. Then it was calculated that the total number of. men employed about the collieries of Durham and Northumberland was 33,990, of whom 15,556 were on the Tyne, 1051 about Blyth, 13,172 on the Wear, and 4211 on the Tees and in South Durham. Now, or at any rate very recently, there were on the books of the Durham Miners' Union alone, 55,000 men ; and in the Northumberland Miners' Association 17,000 men ; the total number of men employed about the collieries of the two counties being estimated at over 123,000. Numerically, therefore, the miners are stronger than they were thirty years ago ; but the experience of recent years, with one or two memorable exceptions, has shown that a suspension of labour, or, indeed, any other form of forcible resistance, is deprecated by the sound and sensible few.

The collieries in the North of England, during the greater part of the time the vend was in existence, were considered equal to producing more than twice the quantity of coal actually required ;* there was, therefore, every inducement to keep up prices by creating a condition of artificial scarcity. But the greatest possible difficulty was found, nevertheless, in keeping the combination together, owing mainly to the impression on the part of some of the colliery owners, that in fixing the quantities to be produced, they were not fairly dealt with. The "regulation" did, as a matter of fact, come to pieces in 1821, and again in 1826, 1829, and 1833. The committee of 1830 found that there were then sixty collieries in the great northern coal-field, and yet when, in 1828, competition was increased by the discontinuance of the regulation, prices fell so low that many collieries suspended operations altogether, and in the opinion of some of the witnesses the then current prices, based on 12s. 9d. per London chaldron † to the coal-owner at the pit's mouth, was required to carry on the trade with any profit. During 1833 the coal trade of the North was open, and at this time, it is stated, coals became so great a drug on the market, that the owners could hardly realise 18s. per Newcastle chaldron for them. This was about 4d. per cwt., or 6s. 8d. per ton. The average selling price of coal in the North has of late years been much less than this, but coal was subject to many charges at that time that it does not now bear. Consumption was greatly

---

* Dunn on the Coal Trade, p. 74.

† The London chaldron theoretically contained 35,569 cubic feet, and weighed 27 cwt. The Newcastle chaldron weighed 53 cwt.

restricted by heavy duties, alike for over-sea and coasting coal. Upon round coal and nuts there was a duty of 17s. per Newcastle chaldron, while the coasting duty was 9s. 4d. on round coal to the 5th April 1824, and 6s. from that date to April 1826. A well-known authority on the trade informed the Parliamentary Committee of 1830, that "if the coasting and foreign duties were abolished, the demand for coal would so increase that regulation would not be wanted." Indeed, in spite of the higher prices induced by the limitation of the output, the cost of producing the diminished quantities was so great that Mr John Buddle, one of the best known colliery engineers of that period, asserted that five per cent. was the average rate of profit earned in the coal trade, after returning the capital.

The frequent break-down and resumption of the combination in the coal trade of the North caused great instability of prices, and great uncertainty in all the operations and prospects of the coal-owners. Thus we find in 1827 the average vend price of what was known as Wear Wallsend was 36s. 6d. per London chaldron; for the next four years, excluding 1829, when there was free trade, the price averaged 34s. 6d. In 1833, free trade reduced the price to 18s., and in 1834 the regulation raised it again to 26s., which, in the following year, was still further raised to 28s. The quantity vended was subject to similar fluctuations. Assuming 1000 tons as a basis, the vend permitted in 1827 was 720 tons; in 1828, 811 tons; in 1830, 835 tons; and in 1834, 645 tons.

The various Parliamentary Committees that sat to inquire into the condition of the coal trade between 1830 and 1836, were apparently greatly perplexed as to the view they should take as to the coal trade combination. Nor is this, perhaps, surprising, considering how conflicting was the character of the testimony offered on the subject. Mr Nicholas Wood, one of the most enlightened and capable men that the coal trade has produced, informed the Committee of 1836, that in his opinion the then price of 26s. per Newcastle chaldron "left an extravagant profit to the coal-owner, and had been one of the causes of the strike among the workmen."* Mr Buddle, on the contrary, stated that since the trade had been regulated, the workmen had given less trouble than before. The Committee of 1836 went no further than to report to Parliament that "the whole system of combination was worthy attention," and recommended that "every means of promoting a new supply be encouraged, as furnishing the most effectual means of counteracting the combinations of the coal-owners and factors." The regulation did not mend as it grew older. Prices continued to fall, in spite of the reduction of output, as the area of competition became widened; and during the three years ending 1843, the collieries in the North were not producing one-half of their normal output. Mr Matthias Dunn wrote in 1844, that "the evil of regulation heretofore has been the limited quantity allowed to each colliery under the abridged trade, but this has been felt more severely by the long-worked and smaller collieries, where, in many instances, the quantity has been so limited, and the price so depressed, that nothing but a losing trade could result; and a strong feeling has prevailed that their relief could only arise from a concession of the quantities disposed of by great and highly-valued collieries for the general good. This feeling has been so urgently advocated

---

* Several strikes of colliery operatives, or "pitmen," took place in the North between 1834 and 1846.

that the present regulation agreement contains a clause for
a general revision and settlement of the basis of every
colliery in the trade—every individual thus satisfying himself with the hope that such general review will benefit him
at the expense of others."

Two of the greatest conceptions of modern times in the
direction of "pools" or "rings" were those projected in the
year 1888 to syndicate the coal trade and the flour trade of
the United Kingdom. These attempts, or rather ideas, for
the matter did not in either case pass beyond the stage of a
proposal—aimed at nothing short of the practical control of
two of the greatest articles of every-day necessity and use,
and they are now mainly interesting in so far as they indicate the bold and daring character of the aims and plans
that are put forward by the syndicate-mongers and ring-
traffickers of these latter days.

The proposal to establish a coal pool that would embrace
and control all the collieries in the United Kingdom, or at
least in Great Britain, was one that not unnaturally attracted
a good deal of attention at the time it was talked about,
although it never went the length of a serious discussion of
terms. A writer in a leading newspaper remarked on the
proposal that the general impression was undoubtedly adverse
to the possibility of founding such a huge monopoly, not
only on the ground of the difficulty of providing the necessary capital to work the scheme, but also on the ground
that it would be practically impossible to obtain the necessary amount of co-operation and cohesion over so wide an
area. There is, however, no insuperable objection on the
first score. There are two ways of working a syndicate of
this kind—it may be worked as the result of a common
agreement among all the parties engaged in the industry

affected, or it may be carried on as the result of the actual acquisition of all the operative works or mines in the country or district to be syndicated. The former is the more general and the more feasible system of the two, and in the case of the rail trade, the sugar trade, and other great trades it has been found to work without much difficulty. The Standard Oil Company in the United States and the Salt Syndicate in this country have, however, proceeded upon somewhat different lines. The first point to be considered is not that of whether there is a possibility of raising a large capital for the purposes in view, but whether there is, in the nature of the case, a probability of securing such a consensus of approval and such a solidarity of interest among the parties concerned as would give the scheme a chance of being launched and carried on with success.

In looking at the question from this point of view, it is necessary to remember, in the first place, that while there is a substantial identity, there is also a great conflict of interests between the different coal-producing districts of the United Kingdom. Steam coal, for example, is produced in Northumberland, South Wales, Scotland, and elsewhere. Coking coal is produced in South and North Durham, in the Midland coal-field, in South Wales, and in one or two other districts. Gas coal is similarly varied in the range of its production. Each district has some special advantages or disadvantages peculiar to itself. One district produces coal cheaper than another; a second district is nearer to the seaboard; another is within easier range of particular markets, and so on. It might, however, be necessary in a pooling arrangement, to disregard these differences, and strike one uniform price for the whole product, whether it was gas, steam, or household coal. The steam coal-owners of South Wales, for instance, might insist on having the same price as their rivals in Northumberland, and *vice versâ*. This uniformity of price would be likely to create grave dissatisfaction, because it would deprive certain districts of the natural advantages which they now enjoy. Not only so, but there would be a constant liability to disagreements on the crucial question of the proportions of the total product of coal that each district and each colliery should supply. If prices were high enough to give a good return, each coal-owner would struggle with might and main to get as high a quota as he could. Those whose proportion was fixed at a lower tonnage than they deemed to be their due would inevitably complain, and secessions would be sure to follow. All this is put on the somewhat large assumption that the coal-owners as a body were favourable to the scheme. But it is difficult to believe that there would be so general an approval of a measure that would have the strongest possible opposition from the outside public, and would, indeed, be likely to demand ultimate Parliamentary interference.

There is, however, something to be said in favour of the proposal to establish a combination in the coal trade. The average price of coal over the last fifteen years, excepting only a short period, has been unremunerative. Very many collieries have been carried on at an absolute loss. Many others have been entirely closed. No one is the richer for the low range of prices. The capitalist is not only not increasing his resources, but he is absolutely dribbling them away. The miners are compelled to work for low wages. The consumer is, indeed, the only one that gains at all by the existing condition of things. Now, it is no doubt a good thing for the consumer to have cheap coal, as it is to have

cheap wheat, and cotton, and sugar, and petroleum ; but there
is this important difference between coal and the other commodities that have been mentioned—coal is almost our sole
indigenous mineral that is of substantial economic value.
On coal we have built up our industrial supremacy ; without
coal our fortunes as an industrial and manufacturing people
would disappear " like the baseless fabric of a vision." It
is, therefore, of great importance that we should make the
best possible use of our coal resources—all the more that
they are of limited extent. But we are not fulfilling this
duty if we allow our coal to be worked out wastefully ; if
we send it abroad in yearly increasing quantities, for almost
the bare cost of production ; if, in a word, we fail to husband our resources, as the Royal Commission of 1869 recommended that they should be husbanded. There is a
possibility that if the collieries of the United Kingdom, as
a whole, were worked under a " trust "—that is, if all the
produce of all the collieries were pooled, so that a certain
fixed price could be depended upon, the trade would be
much the better, and the general community would be very
little the worse. It is, of course, important to premise that
prices should be kept reasonably low ; but they should be
high enough, at the same time, to make it worth the while
of the colliery proprietors to get out the very last ounce of
coal that was available in working ; whereas, under a system
of starvation prices, economy cannot be studied to this
extent, and only the best seams will pay for the cost of
production.

What the increased price ought to be in order to afford
a suitable profit to the coal-owner, and at the same time
avoid injurious results to industry, would, of course, require
to be carefully considered ; and even with the most anxious

consideration of the question, it is probable that upon this rock, sooner or later, the scheme would split. There are, however, other rocks ahead that make the project almost visionary.

The first, and perhaps the most formidable, of all the objects that would be likely to stand in the way of a success-ful coal pool is the enormous variety of individuals and interests that would have to be conciliated. It would not be enough to obtain the consent of two-thirds or three-fourths of the coal trade. There must be a practically unanimous and universal co-operation, or the project would prove to be unworkable. It is of the essence of such a scheme that over-production should be avoided. In order to avoid over-production it would become requisite that the several districts and each colliery should contribute certain fixed proportions to the total quantity of each description of coal required. But this arrangement would provide the opportunity for a firm which, from interested or con-scientious motives, declined to join the pool, to produce to the utmost extent of its capacity, in order to take advantage of the improved price ; and in this way we should probably see a colliery unconnected with the Association working full time, while a larger and better equipped colliery under the "pool" was only working three-quarters time. Then, again, there would be the difficulty of getting the different districts and collieries to accept any possible allotment of their pro-portions. This has always been a serious stumbling-block, and it would certainly prove so again. Of course, it might be possible to starve disaffected and unmanageable concerns into compliance, as was done by the Standard Oil Company in the United States, or, as in the same case, collieries might be bought up or offered a premium to remain idle. But all these are costly expedients, and would be sure to be objected to by a large number of those who "paid the piper."

This statement of the difficulties in the way of the proposed pool may be supported by others equally cogent and obvious.   There are, for example, over 3500 collieries in the United Kingdom as a whole, and as many of these are in the possession of limited liability companies, with large boards of directors, it is likely that, in some cases at least, it would be found impossible to get the consent of all the members of such boards to join the suggested combination.   This has apparently been effected in the case of the salt and chemical pools or rings, but in these cases the area of operations was on a much smaller scale, and the chances of success were proportionately greater.

Again, there can be little doubt that all the railway companies, who are large consumers of coal and coke; the steam shipping companies, who also draw their motive power from the coal trade; the principal industries of the country, and the great body of the people as consumers, would be likely to offer every opposition in their power to such an enterprise.   It would be the coal industry *versus* the world. Is the coal industry strong enough to sustain such a struggle? This is very doubtful indeed.   There are, therefore, likely to be strong external as well as internal influences of a disintegrating character, the complete strength and volume of which could only be got over by something like a miracle.

These considerations are worth while keeping in mind, in view of possible future attempts to " pool " the coal industry of the United Kingdom.   There is a bare possibility that such an attempt may be made.*   The coal trade is one that

* Since these lines were written Sir George Elliott has made a proposal to form a gigantic colliery trust in Great Britain, which is now under consideration.

is little liable to competition from abroad. England can produce the cheapest, as well as the best coal in Europe. It is true that cheaper coal is produced in the United States, but it is a " far cry " to America, and the shipment of a cargo of coals to any large centre of consumption in England would at the very least double its price at the pit's mouth, so that English coal-owners may be said to be entirely relieved from any present fear or danger of foreign competition. If, therefore, the difficulties above referred to could be entirely overcome—if the trade were prepared to stand shoulder to shoulder as one man—there would appear to be no necessarily insuperable difficulty in the way of founding and carrying on a combination to keep up the price of fuel at home, so far as foreign competition is concerned, and this is more than can be said of most other industries.

CHAPTER VI.

TRUSTS IN FOOD PRODUCTS.

IT will hardly be regarded as probable that a ring or syndicate could be formed, and successfully carried on, that could control for a time the price of so indispensable and universal an article as flour, and yet this, and none other, was the end and aim of a ring that was attempted in London in the year 1888.

The syndicate who undertook, or rather began, the undertaking—for it never came into really practical operation—of establishing such a gigantic combination, was not so ambitious as to think of incorporating at once all the flour-milling and flour-selling interests in the kingdom. They began with trying to embrace the whole of the flour trade in the north-east of England—that is to say, the district lying between the Tweed and the Humber. It was attempted, with this end in view, to raise a capital of a million and a half sterling, and in discussing the feasibility of the project, *The Times* remarked that the changes that had, during the last few years, been introduced into the business of flour-milling in the United Kingdom appeared to favour its adoption to a much greater extent than would have been deemed possible previously.

"Down to a very recent period," it was stated, "even four or five years ago, it would have been almost a matter of impossibility to organise a company to monopolise the

68

flour trade. Since that time, however, roller machinery and all the latest milling appliances have, at a large cost, and in some instances on a gigantic scale, been introduced, chiefly by individual capitalists, but to some extent also by limited companies. This has had the twofold effect of driving out of the trade nearly all the smaller country water or steam mills, which ground by the old process from time immemorial, and also of ousting almost entirely the enterprising foreigner, who was rapidly taking possession of the flour market by his being the first to adopt the new system of grinding by the roller process. Capital has been thus, it is alleged, pushed into milling on too liberal a scale, and the gigantic mills put up on the banks of the Tees, Tyne, and at other points have had the effect, at least in a considerable degree, of bringing about over-production, undue competition, and minimised profits. It is with the object of obviating and overcoming such drawbacks to their trade that this great milling syndicate is being formed.

"Considerable ingenuity and not a little plausibility was shown in the presentation of the details of the scheme and the method of organising it. First of all the consumer is, of course, assured that the price of flour, if enhanced at all, will only be raised to an infinitesimal extent. Reliance is chiefly placed on the saving which will be effected in the cost of long railway transit, by dispensing with the large number of salesmen who are constantly pushing the business of the different firms over a wide district, by obviating the storage of wheat in the warehouses at the ports, while something is also to be gained by the prevention of competition. To make the matter clearer, it may be stated that everything appears to hinge on the prevention of competition. Thus, in the matter of railway transit, at present firms in

Newcastle, Stockton, or Darlington send flour over the railway forty to fifty miles to each other's towns. For instance,
Darlington or Stockton send flour to Newcastle, and *vice
versâ*. This will no longer be done. Each district will be
supplied by its own mills. Newcastle will not send to
Stockton, nor Stockton to Newcastle, and the same with
every other portion of the country which the syndicate will
control. The saving in railway carriage and in labour in
loading and unloading under this head is estimated at 9d.
to 1s. per sack on the whole of the production. Then there
will be the advantage of doing without the middleman.
The corn merchant will find his occupation gone. The
syndicate will buy at first hand from the ship or the farmer,
and the grain will be despatched direct to the different
mills. The storage charges which will be dispensed with
are put down at 6d. per sack more. Then there has to be
added the merchants' percentages, travellers' expenses, &c.

"Now the crucial point comes in where the public are
concerned. The saving on 'undue competition,' as it is
termed, is put at 9d. per sack, and this would come out of
the pockets of the consumer. It means, however, less than
a halfpenny per stone of 14 lb. of flour, and will practically,
it is urged, not affect the price of the loaf. The three items
given amount to 2s. per sack, and this alone would yield
the very handsome dividend of about 10 per cent. to the
investors in the new company. There is a consumptive
demand of from 30,000 to 40,000 sacks weekly in the
syndicate's district, and this would give, on 2s. per sack, a
return of £170,000 to £180,000 for dividend. The cost
of working at each individual mill would not need to come
out of the dividend, only the charges for the head office
and directors, as each establishment would not cost more

for management than now, and generally would remain under the present management on behalf of the company.

"The main question for the promoters is, Can the whole trade of the district be brought into the ring? And, next, Can the monopoly be made complete and unassailable? With regard to the first point, it being to their interest to join the syndicate, all the leading millers, or nearly so, have signified their assent. If any should prove recalcitrant, or demand undue value for their property, a little gentle pressure on the part of the syndicate, by cornering them, underselling them in their own district, and by generally making it awkward for them to carry on their trade freely, would, it is asserted, speedily bring them to reason. They could not individually contend against such an organisation as the syndicate, with such vast capital to back it. All the mills, small or large, can, therefore, it is thought, be forced into the ring. Then, with regard to the second point—the establishment and maintenance of the monopoly —the district, it is contended, is unique in itself and can be effectually guarded from outside competition by sea and land. On the land side the ground to be covered is practically conterminous with the North-Eastern Railway on the eastward side — from Berwick to Newcastle, Darlington, York, and Hull. Very large populations are eastward of this area—all the Tyneside district, including Newcastle, Shields, Sunderland, Hartlepools, Middlesbrough, Stockton, Darlington, York, Whitby, Scarborough, Hull, &c.—and there is practically none to the westward of it. The only two points from which competition could come are Leeds and Carlisle, and this would be prevented by the cost of carriage of 1s. to 1s. 3d. per sack. Besides, the syndicate would undersell and drive away competition from any point, if necessary. Outside this area it is proposed to take in Hexham and Barnard Castle, and also Grimsby, on the other side of the Humber, where there are mills. Very little flour is now sent from abroad, and it is considered that it would not pay English millers to forward it from distant ports to the syndicate's district, and in any case they could, if necessary, be undersold. It is thus believed that competition can be warded off, both by sea and land, and the trade thoroughly maintained and controlled.

"The farmers of Northumberland, Durham, and a large part of Yorkshire are hardly likely to regard the syndicate with favour. In their various markets they will, as a matter of fact, only have one customer, who could dictate his own terms, instead of many who now compete for their produce. It is also a matter for consideration by the general British public as to how far such a scheme may be applicable to various parts of the kingdom, as well as the district selected for the operations of the syndicate."

The arrangements for this syndicate proceeded so far that valuers were employed to value the various milling properties between Berwick and Hull, and the price to be paid for each was practically agreed upon.

In the United States, about the same time, similar action was taken by the flour millers in St Louis, and a meeting was held in Milwaukee to discuss the question of a universal restriction of the output of flour, with a view to the keeping up of prices. In 1888 a number of the millers in the State of Minnesota agreed to restrict their output for the remainder of that year—their action being based on the plea that the producing power of the country was largely in excess of the actual practical requirements. This, however, could not, of course, control the operations of farmers in the growing of wheat; and, on the face of it, there would hardly appear to be much to gain in restricting the output of flour if there was a superabundance of wheat, seeing that the wheat might be reduced to flour in other districts, or shipped to Europe for that purpose. At the most, a combination of millers such as that proposed could only exercise a local influence. They could, no doubt, keep up the price of flour in a particular district, but beyond that they would find it impossible to go. Nothing very definite came out of this movement, the difficulties in the way of its consummation having been found insuperable.

Several attempts have, however, been made in the United States to organise combinations for the purpose of regulating the supplies of agricultural produce. When we add that the total agricultural produce of the United States, other than tobacco and cotton, was officially valued for 1891 at 2133 millions of dollars, and that the two articles excepted bring up the total to 2469 millions, it becomes manifest that the regulating of any considerable part of this supply must be an operation of great, if not of unparalleled magnitude.

In March 1888, a movement was started among the farmers of Kansas to found a trust that was intended to include not only wheat growers, but stock raisers and feeders of the North-Western States and Territories of the Mississippi Valley. The *raison d'être* of the trust is set out in the following extract from the address that was circulated by the promoters with a view to its establishment:—

"Within the last ten years the manufacturers, and nearly every other branch of industry except agriculture, have

formed what are termed Trust Associations, having for their
object, first, to check over-production ; second, to prevent
an over-supply of goods being thrown upon our markets to
the ruin of prices and the general injury of trade.   We may
not by this proposed association be able, nor do we care, to
limit the production of the soil, for this will depend more or
less on good and bad seasons ; but we have the power and
can control our shipments, and thus regulate the supply of
our commodities offering in the public markets of the
country, and this will always insure us fair prices.   The
farmers of this country cannot compete with Indian wheat
in the Liverpool market, nor do we intend to longer submit
to the payment of the cost of taking our wheat to Liverpool
before it can be sold in our home market.   What we want
is a fair exchange of products.   This we demand, and will
submit to nothing less.   We have the power, and all that
is needed is organisation to make this power effective.   If
we can by this proposed organisation control our shipment
of these commodities, and prevent the supply from exceeding the demand in the market, then we can unquestionably
become masters of the situation.   The plan contemplates,
first, the establishment of ten central agencies, to wit :
Chicago, Cincinnati, Kansas City, Indianapolis, Omaha, St
Louis, Cedar Rapids, St Paul, Milwaukee, and Louisville ;
these agencies to do all the selling for the members of the
association, for which they shall be paid stated salaries.
Second, the territory tributary to these commercial points
to be divided into eight principal districts, and sub-divided
into sub-districts by counties.   Third, the principal of each
central agency, together with a general superintendent
of the association to be appointed, shall constitute an
executive board, with power to regulate and control ship-

ments of produce upon the markets, and to do any and all other things that shall in their judgment appear to be the best interests of the association."

It seems a pity that the enterprise and originality displayed by the Kansas farmers did not meet with a suitable reward, but as a matter of fact it came utterly to naught. Eighteen months afterwards, however, a convention of the farmers of the Mississippi Valley, called by the Farmers' Federation, was held at St Louis—an organisation of which it was stated at the time that it had "a capital stock of twenty million dollars, of which fifteen millions was in the hands of a trustee to for ever secure farmers in control." In connection with this movement, it was explained,* that "before reaching the consumer, the products of the farms of the Mississippi Valley are charged with ten millions annually paid in commissions," and that "this company proposes to do the selling through salaried agencies for a million dollars."

It was further provided that the dividends earned by the Federation from controlling the wheat business of the south-west were to be used to "establish a bank," "erect grain elevators," and "build stock-yards." Of the $4,500,000 stock not in the hands of a trustee, and for buying out grain commission men, $2,500,000 was to be held "to meet demands for stock that may be earned," presumably among "farmers who do their own shipping, farmers' alliances," &c. Of the $2,000,000 of stock remaining, $500,000 was to be designated privileged stock, subject to such conditions, &c., "as may be imposed." In a reply to inquiry, however, the Vice-President of the Federation stated that only $3000 of the $20,000,000 capital was paid up !

* The *Globe Democrat* of St Louis, October 1889.

The convention comprised one delegate from each county in each state in the Mississippi Valley, and any farmer who raised 500 bushels of wheat in the previous year was to be admitted as delegate likewise.

In the accounts of one of the meetings we find this important statement: "The farmers disclaim any intention of forming a trust; . . . they do not wish to charge exorbitant prices, but simply to regulate the supply to such an extent that the demand will not be so exceeded as to result in disastrous competition." On this point, a leading American journal observed: "This is what most, if not all, the confessed trusts have said. The Federation simulates the trusts, with its trustee holding three-fourths of its stock, even while denying forming a trust." It wants to "establish a uniform price at which wheat shall be sold," and to "regulate the supply, &c.," so that "disastrous competition" will not result. It would be of interest to learn from those engaged in this work—that of saving $9,000,000 commission on wheat for the farmer by buying out the commission merchant—among other things, how this is to be done with the fierce competition from cheap Indian, Russian, and other wheats, seeing that the exportable surplus makes the home price at the seaboard. It really looks as if a crop of competing commission men would be speedily created, and the price to the farmer ultimately be lowered.

The Granger movement was probably the only organisation established in the United States that ever succeeded in the regulation of agricultural produce. But the Granger tried to regulate prices on what the farmer had to buy, whereas the Farmers' Trust proposed to control the prices of what the farmer had to sell. The one appointed agents to buy cheap ; the other proposed to appoint agents to sell produce to the best advantage. The Granger excluded from membership all who were not actually farmers, and was in effect a secret social order, designed not only for commercial purposes, but to accomplish political ends, whereas the Farmers' Trust was declared to be an organisation with " a pocket interest and a business end," and without any secret ties.

Replying to a suggestion that the name of this proposed combination should be changed from that of the Farmers' Trust to that of the Farmers' Protective Union, the president of this Society admitted a prejudice against anything that has the name of " trust " ; but, he added, " this is owing to the fact that the object of a trust is so little understood. A trust is a union of business institutions, and its object is to prevent ruinous competition in trade, experience having demonstrated that competition is not the safe and honest method of doing business. To competition may be traced eighty per cent. of all business failures, and the survival of the fittest or strongest becomes an oppressive monopoly. A trust is a compact between two or more independent business firms, agreeing to do or not to do a certain thing in the line of their business, and implies a trustee to execute the trust, who is restricted or limited to the specific object of the trust. By these modern institutions uniform grades of prices are established, thus protecting the weak against the strong and reserving to each member of the union all the rights and powers not delegated to the trust. A trust, therefore, is decentralising in its influence and a check upon monopoly, the latter being a consolidation of capital or a centralisation of business power, acting under one supreme head, deriving its nourishment and

growth from the failure and ruin of competitors in trade.
When a combination in business assumes this character it
ceases to be a trust and becomes a monopoly.   The manufacturing and commercial classes are organised, but the
agricultural — the fundamental industrial class — is un-
organised and at the mercy of the other two.   The Farmers'
Trust movement, therefore, has become a necessity in order
to secure an equitable exchange of products, and to restore
the normal condition of trade or an equilibrium of production and consumption."

The subsequent history of this remarkable movement I
have been unable to trace with accuracy.   That there
were several combinations founded in reference to American
agricultural produce is beyond question.   The fact of such
a combination existing in the dressed beef trade was
admitted in 1889 to a committee of the United States
Senate, appointed to investigate the subject of cattle and
meat prices and transportation rates, especially in Kansas
and Chicago.   It was also admitted that there had been a
steady decline in the value of beef cattle during the few
prior years without any decline in the price to the consumer,
and that the dressed beef trade was killing the cattle men.
The combination of dressed beef dealers had, it appeared,
agreed that certain prices should be paid for cattle in certain
States.   What those prices were does not appear, but they
were obviously depressed as far as possible, so that the
larger profit might go into the pockets of the purchasers,
the consumer being required to pay for his dressed beef as
much as he did before.

CHAPTER VII.

THE STANDARD OIL TRUST.

PERHAPS the most complete and highly developed of the industrial combinations hitherto attempted is the Standard Oil Trust, a copy of the agreement of whose creators was produced before the New York Senate Committee on Trusts in that city in 1888. The Trust embraces the stock-holders and members of a large number of corporations and partnerships engaged in the production and refining of oil. The parties bind themselves to form corporations under the laws of Ohio, New York, Pennsylvania and New Jersey, and, whenever required by the trustees, to form similar corporations in other states and territories, with the proviso that each corporation shall be known as the Standard Oil Company of such a state or territory. The business of the Trust is managed by trustees, who are empowered, among other things, to "purchase the bonds and stocks of other companies engaged in similar business, and hold the same for the benefit of the owners of the said Trust certificates, and may sell, assign, transfer, and pledge such bonds and stocks whenever they may deem it advantageous to the said Trust so to do." The Trust is, under the agreement, to continue during the lives of the survivors and survivor of the trustees, and for twenty-one years thereafter, though provision is made whereby its affairs may be wound up, if necessary, at an earlier time. The original capital of the Trust was

$70,000,000, and it was afterwards increased to $90,000,000. About $30,000,000 of its capital is invested in pipe lines. It recently refined about 75 per cent. of the American oil product. The Trust, as will be seen from this description, is not a corporation, but rather a federation of corporations. The existence of such a gigantic combination shows to what an extent the play of competition, as an element in business, is being destroyed or rendered ineffective.

The leading spirit, and the President, since its establishment, of the Standard Oil Company is Mr John D. Rockefeller, who some thirty years ago was clerk in a produce commission house in Cleveland, Ohio. When the discovery and development of the oil-fields of Pennsylvania, about 1864-65, led to a speculative excitement in that State, he and his partner purchased some of the oil-bearing land then in the market, and tried the experiment of refining crude petroleum. In this aim he had the co-operation of Samuel Andrews, who had been a day labourer in oil refineries, and who improved upon the experience gained in this capacity by introducing a system of refining which yielded more kerosene than could be obtained from petroleum by any other system then practised.

Rockefeller and his partner, Clark, were so satisfied with the results of the system proposed by Andrews, that they constructed, with the aid of borrowed capital, an oil refinery in order to put the system into practical operation. The experiment succeeded, and Rockefeller persuaded his brother William to go into the business. A second refinery was started, and the two having been consolidated under one management, the owners were able to produce refined oil, not only on a considerable scale, but at a cheap cost. A warehouse was meanwhile opened in New York for the sale of the refined product, for which there was a large demand at prices that left a handsome profit.

The Rockefellers had, however, comparatively little capital, and at this juncture the development of their business was aided materially by the co-operation of Mr Henry M. Flagler, who became a partner, and introduced 60,000 dollars of capital into the venture. This gave an immediate impulse to the concern, and led to the starting of the Standard Oil Company, in which the Rockefellers, Andrews, and H. M. Flagler were the original partners. The capital stock of the company, as originally formed, was only a million dollars. The company had not long been established when it began to buy up and crush out rival concerns. Some of the owners of these concerns received a fair cash price for their properties ; others were paid with Standard Oil Company's stock. But, however dealt with, all were made to feel the influence of the Standard Company, which, within seven years of its foundation, had secured a practical monopoly of the refined oil business of the United States, and which, for years past, has been the largest industrial corporation in the United States, if not in the world. The development of such a gigantic business from an original investment, in 1864, of 75,000 dollars, by four young and unknown men, is a striking example of the singularly fruitful results of enterprise and business capacity that every now and again occur to stimulate and encourage those who possess such qualifications and know how to apply them. It need hardly be added that the four young men referred to have become enormously wealthy.* They have, more-

* John D. Rockefeller is supposed to be the richest man in the United States, and his fortune is stated at about 125 millions of dollars. His annual income is reported to be six millions of dollars, or

over, become wealthy—strange as the statement may appear
—without any increase in the price of the products dealt in
by the combination.   On the contrary, it is contended that
since the company was established the price of oil has
steadily fallen, until for some years past it has been much
lower than was ever dreamt of before its formation.

This remarkable fact has been stated so clearly and with
such adequate explanation in a recent pamphlet, that we
cannot do better than reproduce the words of the writer* :—

"1. *The Standard Oil Combination has not withheld
supplies and increased prices, but the contrary.*—The oil
business began in 1859.   This co-operation of refiners
began in 1872, but reached no considerable proportions
until 1874.

"In 1873 the production of oil was about five million
barrels, and consumption about equal.   Price of crude oil
at well, $3.86 per bbl.   Price of export oil in New York,
barrel included, $11 per bbl.

"In 1873, the first year after co-operation began, the production of oil reached nearly ten million barrels, the consumption was nine and one-half millions, the price of crude
oil fell to an average of $1.73 per bbl., and the price of
export oil to $7.50 per bbl.   The value of exports, notwith-
standing the decrease in price, increased from thirty-two
and a half millions to forty-two millions of dollars.

"In 1876 there was a rise in the price of crude oil to
an average of $2.50 per bbl., based upon the fact that pro-

£1,250,000 sterling !   It has been said that "neither the Astors, with
their vast real estate investments, nor Jay Gould, with his great railroad possessions, nor the richest of the Vanderbilt heirs, can show up
such a bank account as his."

* Mr S. C. T. Dodd, solicitor to the Trust.

duction was not materially increasing, and the oil regions, then confined to Venango, Clarion, and Butler counties, Pennsylvania, were supposed to be fully developed and liable to exhaustion. Refined oil advanced in consequence to an average of $8.00 per bbl. for that year. From that date the increase in supply and decrease in price has been constant. At the close of 1881, the date of formation of the Trust, the consumption of oil had increased to over nineteen million barrels per year; the price of export oil at New York had increased to about $3.36 per bbl., which, estimating package at $1.50 per bbl., leaves $1.86 as the price of the oil per barrel, and yet the value of the exports amounted to over forty million dollars, showing an enormous increase in the trade.

" Notwithstanding the wonderful decrease in price and increase in amounts supplied to the market up to this time, let us see what followed the creation of the Trust. The decrease in price and increase in supplies did not cease. At the close of 1887, six years after the creation of the Trust, we find the supply to the markets increased to over twenty-six and a half millions of barrels, of forty-two gallons each, per year : the price of the crude material reduced to an average of 66.66 cents per barrel, and the price of 110° Standard White to $2.81 per bbl. of fifty gallons, including the barrel. And notwithstanding the almost nominal price of oil, the value of exported products reached for that year the enormous sum of $46,824,933. . . .

" It is said the decrease in the price of refined products is entirely in consequence of the decline in the price of crude oil. If so, the Standard can claim no credit for it, because the result of all its operations is to keep up the price of the crude product. But look at the figures. In 1872 crude oil was 9.43 cents per gallon and refined 23.59 cents per gallon. In 1887 crude oil was 1.59 cents per gallon, or 7.84 cents less than in 1872. Had the refined product been reduced only to the same extent it would have been 15.75 cents per gallon in 1887. But it was only 6.72 cents per gallon. The difference, 9.03 cents per gallon, represents the reduction in the refined products after eliminating the effect of the decline in crude. The prices of all other products of petroleum were reduced in the same proportion, and as over a thousand million gallons of crude were consumed in 1887, *this reduction in the cost of refined products, after allowance for the reduction in crude, benefited the public to the extent of about* ONE HUNDRED MILLIONS OF DOLLARS for that single year. For this the Standard claims its due proportion of credit.

" 2. *Cheapening Transportation.*—In 1872 the pipe line system was in its infancy. A number of local lines existed. Their service was inefficient and expensive. There was no uniform rate. The united refiners undertook to unite and systematise this business. They purchased and consolidated the various little companies into what was long known as the United Pipe Line System. The first effect of this combination was a reduction of price of all local transportation to a uniform rate of at first 30 and soon after 20 cents per barrel. The pipes were placed at every well. A storage system was also adopted. Huge iron tanks were built in which oil could be stored awaiting a market. The cost of storage has been reduced until it is now cheaper than that of any other commodity. Oil was taken from any well, stored in these tanks, and a certificate given to the producer, showing the amount. These certificates ultimately became the medium of trade in oil. They were bought and sold, and when presented at any pipe line terminus at any railroad the oil was delivered on board cars. The amount of capital behind these certificates, and the uniformly careful manner in which the business was conducted, eventually created such public confidence in them that they have been dealt in by thousands of persons in this and other countries who never saw a barrel of crude oil. Exchanges for their sale exist in several of the principal cities. They are taken by banks as collateral. They are as good as money. They are now dealt in in the New York Stock Exchange. Oil is delivered on them in New York as well as in the oil region.

"Although the business was built up and owned by those who built up and own the Standard Oil Company, the business is done for the public. Its benefit to the oil trade has been incalculable. Instead of, as is sometimes charged, the Standard being the sole buyer, the buyers are numbered by thousands. The producer not only gets the highest possible price which competition to purchase will bring; he gets also cash in hand. He never sees his oil from the moment it leaves his well. When he wants his well tank relieved, he telephones a pipe line gauger, sees his oil pumped, receives a ticket showing the amount, takes it to a pipe line office, and gets a certificate which he can hold, borrow on, or sell in any exchange, as he sees fit. No one can estimate this advantage to the business. Without combination, aggregated capital, and public confidence in the security, it could not have been accomplished. Should you dissolve the combination, and disperse the capital which makes these certificates secure, the system could no longer be maintained.

"The figures will show that in one year the production of

oil exceeded thirty-one millions of barrels, or nine million barrels in excess of consumption. Consider for a moment what this means. Every day of that year iron tankage had to be built to accommodate twenty-five thousand barrels of surplus oil. This meant an army of iron workers and tank builders, and a cost per day of $7500. . . .

"About 1879 or '80, it was discovered that railways were inadequate to the task of getting oil to the seaboard as rapidly as needed. Combined capital and energy were equal to the emergency. No need to detail how it was done. To-day there reaches from the oil regions of Pennsylvania and New York to the principal cities iron pipes conducting oil as it comes from the wells. Two such lines reach to New York harbour, with a capacity of 25,000 barrels per day. There is one such line to each of the cities of Philadelphia, Baltimore, Buffalo, Cleveland, and Pittsburgh, built by the Standard Oil Combination at a cost of millions, and doing business for the public.

"Now, a word as to railway transportation. The one burden of the charges against the Standard is, that it received special rates from railroads, which enabled it to distance its competitors. There is more grounds for this than any other charge made against it. As before remarked, probably the necessity of in some way improving and cheapening transportation was a strong inducement to the original combination. There were competing roads, and it was found that those who could ship in large and uniform quantities over any particular road could command special rates. It was then the universal mode of business. The man who could not avail himself of it might as well retire from business. The Standard availed itself of this mode of dealing. It could furnish the railroads with, not car loads, but train loads. Besides, it built loading stations, and loaded the trains by its own labour. It built terminal stations, where it received and unloaded trains itself. It became its own insurer, and released the railroads from any obligations for damages. It found that the country had not white - oak forests sufficient to furnish material for making barrels to hold all the oil shipped, and it experi- mented on car after car for carrying oil in bulk. When the proper car was found, it constructed thousands of them, and placed them on the railroads. For these services it demanded and obtained low and lower rates of freight. The freight was lowered to the public at the same time. In 1872, it cost $1.50 to get a barrel of oil to New York. To-day it costs 50 cents.

"It is true the Standard often got a special rate. The railroads refused to carry oil for the same prices for those who shipped in packages in car-load or less than car-load lots, who did not do their own loading or unloading, or furnish their own cars or terminal facilities. Whether this was an absurd, unjust, and criminal position for the rail- roads to take, let the Supreme Court of the United States decide. The question in various phases is before it. The Standard has always contended that its immense outlay in cheapening the actual cost to the railroads of oil transporta- tion entitled it to correspondingly less rates of freight. . . .

" 3. *Cheapening the Cost of Manufacture.*— The Associa- tion of Refiners united the best knowledge and skill in the business. If one had a patent it was open to all. If one had a secret the others shared it. Methods were compared. New plans were tested. Results were and are carefully collated. If one establishment succeeds in saving the fraction of a cent. per barrel in making oil, the reason is known and the method of saving adopted. If good results are obtained in one manufactory and bad results in another, the reason is at once discovered and faults corrected. Scientific men are constantly employed who have made useful discoveries in new products and new methods of manufacture. The consequence of all this is that since 1872 the actual cost of manufacture of refined oil has been reduced 66 per cent. The public have the advantage of this in the reduced price at which the oil is sold, which benefit amounts to millions annually.

4. " *The Same Cheapening of Manufacture* has taken place in the manufacture of barrels, tin cans, boxes for enclosing cans, paint, glue, and acid.

" In 1872 barrels cost the trade $2.35 each. They are now manufactured at our own manufactories at a cost of $1.25 each. About 3,500,000 barrels are used per annum. This single item amounts to $4,000,000 per year.

"In 1874 cans cost 30 cents each. They are now made by our manufactories for less than 15 cents.

"Thirty-six million cans are used each year, and this one item of saving amounts to $5,400,000 each year.

" In 1874 wooden cases cost 20 cents each. They are now manufactured by our own manufactories at a cost of about 13 cents each. The saving in this item alone amounts to $1,250,000 each year.

"The same cheapening process has taken place in the manufacture of tanks, stills, pumps, and everything used in the business.

"All these millions are saved by the economies which combination of persons, capital, experience and skill render possible, without reducing the wages of a single labouring man.

" 5. *The Business in By-Products of Petroleum.*—After illuminating oil is manufactured a large residuum is left. Up to 1875 this was almost exclusively used as fuel at the refineries. The Standard devoted especial attention to this residuum. Experts visited the great shale works in Scotland and studied their methods. The consequence was that extensive works were erected for the manufacture of products from this residuum, principally lubricating oils and paraffin wax. These works are necessarily expensive, and manufacture the residuum of a large number of refineries. Small refineries cannot advantageously engage in this branch of business, and cannot afford to manufacture illuminating oils unless they can dispose of their residuum. This is one of the reasons so many small refineries prove failures. The cost of manufacture of lubricating oils and wax has been reduced by improved methods and constant attention, and the price to the consumer has been constantly reduced, averaging to-day fifty per cent. less than in 1878.

" The use of illuminating oils was introduced to the public with comparative ease, because it met an urgent need. Lubricating oils, on the contrary, met with slow recognition, having to supplant sperm, lard, and fish oils. In Europe, in addition, the products of shale had to be competed with. The work was pushed with vigour, with capital, and with success. An enormous home and foreign trade has been established in these by-products.

" Numerous other useful products are obtained from petroleum, and no expense has been spared to find a use and a market for them. All this results in ability to sell illuminating oil at a price a little above the cost of the crude product, and thus to make it 'the poor man's light.'

" 6. *Markets for Products.*—To make the consumption as

great as it is, the first essentials were good quality and cheapness. But that is not enough. Twenty-five years ago the world was just beginning to hear of Petroleum. When this Standard Combination was formed twelve years had elapsed and the world was using less than six millions of barrels per annum. Of that three and one-half million barrels were exported. In two years afterwards the exports were nearly six million barrels. The reason for it was that no single refinery could afford to keep agents in Europe and Asia to demonstrate the advantages of this product, open means for its convenient and safe transhipment, and force it upon the trade. The refiners when combined could do it, did do it, and continue to do it. The consequence is that petroleum is to-day the light of the world. It is carried wherever a wheel can roll or a camel's hoof be planted. The caravans on the desert of Sahara go laden with Pratt's Astral, and elephants in India carry cases of Standard White. Ships are constantly loading at our wharves for Japan, Java, and the most distant isles of the sea. Our country's revenues are swollen fifty millions of dollars per year by this trade. Think you it was built up or maintained without cause? It never could have happened without combination of persons and capital, and without the support of combination and capital the whole trade would be swept to destruction as the vanishing of a cloud on a summer's day. To illustrate, let me give the history of a small subject.

"Complaints occasionally come to us from all parts of the world that oil is not proving satisfactory. An agent is sent to investigate. Sometimes the cause of the trouble is found to be Russian oil in American packages, or oil under false trade-marks. Consuls, Ministers, and Governments are besieged until a remedy is obtained. One great cause of complaint arose from bad wicks. Some years ago a manufactory was established by the Standard interests for manufacturing the best wick known. Its capital is large, but it sinks about all its capital every year. The wicks are sold at a price so low as to compel their use. Things like these cost thousands of dollars per annum, but they save our market. This is done at our expense, but our competitors reap their share of the benefit. Without combination it would not be done at all."

The remarkable success that attended the earlier operations of the Standard Oil Company has been generally attributed to the fact that its managers succeeded in securing from many of the trunk railroads of the United States special rates of transportation. The power which it had for several years exerted as an evener in the coal-oil pool between the trunk lines extending from the oil regions to the sea-board, had enabled it to secure a monopoly of that traffic. It thereby became almost the only purchaser and shipper of crude petroleum in those regions, and, simultaneously, it became almost the only proprietor of a system of pipe lines ramifying into all parts of the oil districts, whereby the oil is conveyed to tanks belonging to or controlled by that company, and to tanks belonging to producers and dealers in crude petroleum. As a result of these extraordinary advantages, the Standard Oil Company became almost the only refiners of petroleum, and in 1879 it was estimated that 95 per cent. of all the coal-oil refined in the United States was refined by that company.* For a number of years also it was almost the only shipper of oil from the

* Report on the Internal Commerce of the United States for 1879, p. 179.

producing regions to the sea-board, which gave it a control over the entire exports of petroleum from the United States.

One remarkable result of the extensive operations and influence of the Standard Oil Company was that it virtually controlled the production and price of oil and petroleum products all over the world. This means, of course, that the corporation got the mineral oil industry of Scotland under its thumb. But if it was strong, the company was also merciful. So far from competing with the important industry which is engaged in the distillation of oil and paraffin from the shales of Bathgate, the Standard Company struck up an offensive and defensive alliance with the Scotch refiners, and that arrangement has now been in operation for several years. But at one time it certainly looked as if the Standard Company were likely to crush the Scotch mineral oil industry out of existence. That industry, although for many years after it was founded by the late Mr James Young of Glasgow enjoying a high degree of prosperity, had fallen upon evil times in consequence of the competition of American products on the one hand and Russian on the other. But it has enjoyed a greater measure of success since the alliance or arrangement with the Standard Company was established, than it had had for a number of years previously. This is a result of carrying out the policy approved by George Stephenson, when he told a Parliamentary Committee that "where combination is possible competition is impossible." Nor have the consumers suffered in consequence.

An English journal stated in 1889, that "the Scotch and American oil producers have extended the agreement entered into a year ago for another term. In the main the new agreement is similar to the old, and it is to hold good till 1890 at least." A Scotch journal stated, in 1892, that, " as before, the minimum prices have been fixed at what is conceived to be a moderate level, so that consumers will have no reason to look upon the combination as one designed to bear heavily on them. All parties to the arrangement, indeed, are actuated by the proper desire to popularise, so to speak, the products of the trade, and the policy now assured will attain that object. A year ago, when the prices fixed on by the association for burning oil and scale were first heard of, black ruin was pictured as in store for those concerned. Instead of that the year has been a splendid one for the trade, as will be demonstrated when the annual balances are made up, for whereas in the spring of 1888 only three companies divided any money among their shareholders, this year not more than two, probably, will appear in the black list. And should present counsels prevail, the position will be even better a year hence. While the Scotch companies have thus a more favourable outlook, the certificates of the Standard Oil Trust have declined in value during the past six months. The competition of Russian oil is telling, and the effect would be still greater if pipe lines were laid down from Baku to Batoum, as the present means of transport by railway is both slow and costly."

In spite, however, of the claims put forward on behalf of the Standard Oil Trust, it never enjoyed popularity, and decisions given against it in several leading American courts —notably in that of Ohio—threatened to jeopardise its very existence. Hence it was deemed desirable that the Trust should be dissolved, and this was done in March 1890, by a vote of the certificate holders at a meeting called for the purpose. The resolutions dissolving the Trust provided that the agreement, dated January 2, 1882, be terminated ; that the affairs of the Trust be wound up by eight trustees named, or their survivors ; that these trustees have power to act by a majority of their number, to fill any vacancies therein, to sign all papers by one or more of their number as attorneys in fact ; that they report from time to time to the parties interested all transactions had or done by virtue of the resolutions ; and that the power to vote upon any stocks standing in the name of the trustees shall cease at the end of four months from the date of the dissolution.   The resolutions further provided that all property held by the Trust, except stocks of corporations, shall be sold by the trustees at private sale, and the proceeds thereof, together with any money belonging to the Trust, shall be distributed to the owners of Trust certificates according to their respective interests, and that all stocks of corporations held by the trustees shall be distributed to the owners of Trust certificates in proportion to the respective equitable interests of such owners in the stocks so held in trust as evidenced by the Trust certificates.

In explanation of this latter provision, it is declared that each owner of a Trust certificate or certificates shall be entitled to deliver such certificate or certificates for cancellation, and to receive in lieu thereof an assignment of as many shares or fractions of shares in each of the corporations whose stocks are held in the Trust as he is entitled to by virtue of such certificate or certificates, it being declared to be the intent and meaning of the provision that the equitable interests in the stocks represented by Trust certificates may thus on demand be converted into legal interests represented by assignments and transfers of such stocks by the trustees to the parties entitled thereto.   Furthermore, all purchases, sales, exchanges, and cancellations of stocks or agreements therefor made by the trustees during the existence of the Trust, were ratified and confirmed. The thirty companies were to be consolidated or reduced to eighteen, in doing which, according to a statement made by Mr Dodd, the solicitor of the Trust, it was proposed to leave in each state only one company, which was intended to control all the refineries in that state owned by the Standard Company.

A good deal of testimony was given before the House Committee on Manufactures in 1888, tending to show that the Standard Oil Trust kept down and greatly injured rival dealers. One witness declared that the Trust received from the railway companies fourth-class rates on quantities of oil in less than car-load rates, whereas he had to pay first-class rates, and that he had practically been driven out of business in localities covered by certain roads who thus favoured the Trust.

It has been denied by the Trust that it was established to diminish output or raise prices, but it was admitted before the Committee of the House of Representatives that by a contract with the Oil Producers' Association, the production of crude oil was to be curtailed by 17,500 barrels a-day, at the least. It was not denied that the prices of the commodities dealt in had fallen since the Trust was established, but the House Committee contended that this "was due, not to the existence of the Trust, but to the extension of the field of oil production and the ever-increasing volume of crude oil put upon the market," while the Trust had only lowered the price to the consumer to serve their own purposes, being compelled thereto by the increasing supply. It was, moreover, pointed out that the Trust had doubtless the power to put up prices, even if that power was not exercised.

It would be natural to expect that the Standard Oil Trust should become a vast source of wealth to those who controlled and owned the properties syndicated. And so, no doubt, it was at one time. The secretary of the organisation informed the House Committee on Manufactures in 1888 that the market value of the stock of the Trust was 144 million dollars, or about 28 millions sterling; that the average net earnings had been 13 per cent.; and that the average dividends had been 7 per cent. It will hardly be contended that the latter was an exorbitant rate, although it is probable that large sums were carried to reserve, and the value of the property thereby greatly appreciated.

There is something of a parallel between the Standard Oil Company of our own times and the Hanseatic League, although six centuries intervene between them. The origin of the Hanseatic confederacy has been referred by Hallam, in point of time, to the middle of the thirteenth century, and it was founded on the necessity of mutual defence.* The Standard Oil Trust was a confederation, not of cities, but of manufacturers, and was also founded on the necessity of defence—not from " piracy by sea and pillage by land," but from the almost equally disastrous consequences of over-production, and low or impossible profits. "The League had four principal factories in foreign parts—at London, Bruges, Bergen, and Novogorod;"† the Standard Oil Trust had factories in a number of the principal American States, and largely controlled kindred factories in Europe.‡ The principal cities of the Hanseatic com-

---

* Hallam's "Middle Ages," vol. ii. p. 388.   † Hallam, *op. cit.*
‡ It has been shown that the prices at which mineral oil and

bination, "having the command of all the markets in England, with joint or united stocks, they broke all other merchants." * The great outcry against the Standard Oil Trust has made much of the fact that they had such resources as enabled them to virtually swamp all other manufacturers and dealers in the same business. The Hanseatic League "were also accused of having frequently exceeded the bounds of even the great privileges granted to them ; yet by the force of great presents they had purchased new grants; they traded in a body, and thereby undersold and ruined others." † Precisely the same charges have been made against the Standard Oil Trust. The Hanseatic League, in consequence of their great wealth and influence, secured a controlling voice in the shipping trade, and were able to obtain cheaper freights than others, which materially assisted their business operations. The Standard Oil Company has gone a long way in the same direction, so far as American railway transport is concerned. Finally, in 1552, the English Parliament ordered "that all the liberties and privileges claimed by, or pretended to be granted to, the merchants of the House, are void by the laws of this realm," and yet the League continued long afterwards to enjoy a prosperous career, with still continued special privileges and immunities, whereas the Standard Oil Trust, after having been virtually declared illegal and in restraint of trade by adverse decisions in the law courts of the United States, continues not only to enjoy a corporate existence, but to transact an enormous business in all the principal countries of the world, including Great Britain.

paraffin products were sold by the Scotch manufacturers were controlled by this organisation.

* Macpherson's "Commerce," vol. ii. p. 109.

† *Ibid.*, vol. ii. p. 109.

CHAPTER VIII.

THE COTTON-SEED OIL TRUST.

THE Cotton-Seed Oil Trust introduces us to one of the most striking examples to be found in the annals of modern industry of the development of a gigantic business from a previously waste product. Little more than thirty years ago, only some half-a-dozen cotton-seed oil mills existed in the United States. The article, indeed, was comparatively unknown, and hardly at all used. So recently, indeed, as 1883, the total quantity of cotton-seed oil exported from the United States was no more than 415,000 gallons. From that point, however, the industry advanced with a giant's strides. In 1884, the exports were fully eight times as much as they had been in the previous year. In 1885, they were nearly double what they had been in 1884; but from this period they appear to have fluctuated in a very irregular way; for whereas they only reached 2,690,700 gallons in 1889, they rose in the following year to the enormous figure of about $13\frac{1}{2}$ million gallons, or nearly four times as much as in the previous year. No other vegetable oil is so largely exported from either the United States or any other country. The quantity of cotton-seed oil used in America may be at least equal to the quantity exported, so that its manufacture has become a large and important industry, which has turned out very serviceable

for the commercial interests of the Southern States, previously far from prosperous.

Bradstreet's, of the 30th October 1886, remarks on the
Cotton-Oil Trust that "the fact that a fine oil could be
extracted from cotton-seed was known long ago, and pointed
out as a possible source of large revenue to the cotton-pro-
ducing States. Its development, however, into a larger
industry is a matter of comparatively recent date. Some
few years ago the business commenced to assume large
dimensions. Mills sprang up in every section of the cotton
states, and the oil took its place as a product of value, involving the utilisation of what had in the main been previously
largely waste. It may be stated at this point that many
authorities on the subject contend that this utilisation of
the cotton-seed tends to unduly impoverish the soil, and
that a true economy on the part of the planter would
demand its return to the ground. This, in fact, is known
to be practised by many careful planters, but it is certain
that the greater part of the seed product was and still is put
to no use whatever. The proportion of seed to the cotton
is about half a ton to a bale of cotton; in other words,
with a cotton crop of 7,000,000 bales, the total seed would
be some 3,500,000 tons, of which the requirements for
planting purposes would be but 5 per cent., leaving
3,300,000 tons for fertilising or crushing. How much of
it has been turned to the latter use it is not easy to state,
but the best estimates are that in the last few years the
amount so employed has been between 450,000 and
600,000 tons yearly. The number of mills has been stated
to be as high as 200, and in addition there are a number
of refineries. The average price of the crude oil is about
30 cents. per gallon, but no definite statistics have been

attainable of late as to the total product of oil and oil-cake, or its value.   The statement is made that if all the seed was utilised for crushing purposes it would add some 30 per cent. to the value of the cotton product."

These considerations furnish some approximate means of judging of the character and extent of the cotton-seed oil industry.   Owing to the rapidity with which the industry was developed, a large product was thrown upon the market, and prices fell to a point which was declared to be unremunerative, and which appeared likely to throw obstacles in the way of the future growth of the business.   In these circumstances, a number of the more enterprising owners of mills and refineries in the several States decided to form a Trust to regulate production.   About seventy different corporations joined the organisation, which was founded, as regards its management, its relation to, and control of, the companies whose stock was held by its nine trustees, on much the same lines as the Sugar Trust, elsewhere referred to (p. 107).   The articles of agreement made provision for taking into the syndicate new competitors upon the original terms.

The Trust, it seems, was largely based upon the ownership of a patent process for cleaning cotton-seed preparatory to crushing.   Under the old process, since the lint adhering to the seed could not be entirely removed, it was necessary to cut the seed in two, extract the kernel, and press the oil out of it only.   The shell and adhering lint were used as fuel or thrown away.   Some years ago a simple and economical chemical process was invented, by which the lint can be freed from the seed, leaving it perfectly clean, like an apple-seed, and enabling it to be crushed whole, thus increasing the products about 50 per cent.   The difference

in results between the old and the new processes are said to
be nearly as follows :—

Formerly there was obtained from one ton of seed—

36 gallons oil at 30 c., ...	$10.80
750 pounds oilcake at 1¼ c.	9.37
30 pounds cotton at 5 c., ...	1.50
	$21.67

The product of the new process would be—

50 gallons oil at 30 c., ...	$15.00
1600 pounds oilcake at 1 c., ...	16.00
30 pounds cotton at 5 c., ...	1.50
	$32.50

The oilcake produced by the new process contains the
shells, and as it is not so rich as the old process cake, it
is worth a little less.   This is, however, claimed as an
advantage, since the new process cake is not too rich for
use as feed without any mixture with bran or other feed.

The patents covering that process came into the hands
of parties who saw their value as a key to the mastery of
the business.   A thorough investigation was made, and a
number of capitalists became interested themselves in the
scheme, including, it is said, some of the leading members
of the Standard Oil Trust, upon the lines of which the
Cotton-Seed Oil Trust was organised, and commenced
operations.   The effort at the start was to get control of
the best factories.   Negotiations were opened with their
owners, and the properties were appraised and sold to the
Trust.   It is reported that the original purchases were on
the basis of $350 in its certificates for each $100 of the
estimated cash value.

The start once made, the Trust proceeded to acquire other mills, although the prices paid were much lower than at first, until it had about all it needed. Some of the concerns which were left out afterwards applied to be admitted. One of the principles of the Trust has been to have the proprietors who came into the Trust still operating their mills as superintendents, under the direction of the combination. This method was found to act as an inducement to owners to sell, and also tended to cloak the operations of the Trust.

According to the Census of 1880, the total capital employed in the cotton-seed oil mills of the United States was returned at some four million dollars. Six years afterwards, when the Trust was established, the issue of certificates issued to the companies entering into the combination represented a par value of about nine times that amount; and even then the Trust did not embrace more than 70 per cent., if so much, of the producers. Hence it appears to be probable that a large part of the nominal capital was what the Americans euphemistically describe as "water." An estimate made in a leading commercial journal in 1888 placed the daily capacity of the mills in the hands of the Trust at about 9000 tons of seed, but many of the smaller concerns were not included in its operations.

Although, as has been stated, the real aim of the organisation was to regulate production and price, the Cotton-Seed Oil Trust does not appear to have been particularly successful in either. The President of the Trust—Mr J. H. Flagler—has claimed,[*] that the operations of the combination have been attended with great advantage to the industry,

* "Trusts: An Address delivered before the Commercial Club of Providence, Rhode Island, December 1888."

and have largely aided in its development. He also claims that, under the Trust, while the average price of cotton-seed (which represents the amount paid to the Southern farmer) has largely increased, and the quality of the product has been improved, the price has been reduced. Ten years previously to the year 1888, the average price of "summer yellow oil was about 48 cents a gallon ; the year before the Trust the average price was about 47 cents per gallon ; thus it had fallen an average of one cent in five years. In 1887, however, it had fallen to an average of about 39 cents per gallon, showing an average reduction in price of eight cents per gallon during the four years of the Trust ; that is, the price during the four years of the Trust has been reduced by eight times more than it was during the five years before the Trust." Mr Flagler continues—"Not only to the individual is there the benefit of a reduced price, but this great industry gives employment to thousands of our citizens, opens a new field for capital and labour, brings to our homes a new, healthful, and most desirable article of diet, and develops the internal resources of our great country. It takes on the dignity of a national concern, and I do not hesitate to say that this development would have been utterly impossible under the old forms of business organisation. The experience of the twenty-five years pre-ceding demonstrated this, for the business was in a languishing, unsettled, and depressed condition, two-thirds of the corporations whose stockholders have formed this Trust being at the time practically bankrupt, giving only spasmodic employment, and living only a feeble and uncertain existence."

It would naturally be expected that an institution that had conferred such obvious advantages upon the community as Mr Flagler here claims, would be acclaimed as a thing to be encouraged and conserved. But Mr Flagler evidently did not make due allowance for the perversity of the human mind, and especially for the characteristic ingratitude of mankind. The Trust was denounced on all hands, and from first to last its almost meteoric career was a continuous struggle against unpopularity, opposition, and financial troubles, until it was decided that the only course left open was to dissolve the organisation.

So great had the opposition to the action of the Trust become that it was seriously proposed that the planters should institute a "boycott" against it on a grand scale, and refuse altogether to sell it their cotton-seed. This proposition met with some favour, but the difficulty of carrying it out is obvious. On the other hand, the claim was made on behalf of the Trust that the trouble all proceeded from a class of middle-men, whom the Trust had endeavoured to get rid of by organising its own purchasing agencies, and endeavouring to reach the producers directly. These middlemen, it was said, were accustomed to buy seed from the farmers at low figures, about $3 per ton, and re-sold it to the manufacturer at a price which left a handsome profit above the cost of transporting it to the mill. The Trust, it was claimed, would pay the farmer a better price than the middleman would, but the latter, naturally, fought against being abolished. The preponderance of evidence seemed to point to the exercise by the Trust of considerable oppression towards the producers. It was further objected that Standard Oil methods had been copied with reference to the railroads, combinations having been made with them and rates obtained which prevented the few independent mills from using the roads, either for obtaining seed or for transporting their product in competition with the Trust.

According to Professor Jenks,* the Cotton-Seed Oil Trust only declared one dividend of 4 per cent., payable in quarterly instalments, and of this dividend only one instalment was ever paid. It was, however, reported in 1890 that its profits were not far from 11 per cent. to certificate holders who bought at 33 per cent. During the last five years of the existence of the Trust its certificates fluctuated enormously in price, showing their extremely speculative character. In 1887 they touched a maximum of $63\frac{3}{4}$ and a minimum of $29\frac{1}{2}$; in 1888 they varied between $55\frac{1}{4}$ and $27\frac{3}{4}$; in 1889, between $58\frac{1}{2}$ and 31; while, in 1890, the ordinary certificates fell to $15\frac{1}{2}$. After the Trust had been dissolved, it was reorganised as the American Cotton Oil Company, but since then, at any rate up to about a year ago, no dividends have been declared.

* "Trusts in the United States," in the *Economic Journal* for March 1892.

CHAPTER IX.

THE SUGAR TRUST IN THE UNITED STATES.

IT does not appear so difficult a matter to understand how an organisation may be established and carried on successfully for the purpose of controlling a commodity that is more or less indigenous to the country, and which, being always cheap and abundant, is not subject to foreign competition to any material extent. It would, however, appear to be otherwise with a commodity that is not indigenous, and the supplies of which are mainly obtained from foreign countries. There is this material difference to be observed between the Standard Oil Trust and the Sugar Trust—the second most important founded in the United States.

In the import business of the United States, sugar has for many years appeared to be the most important item. For the last twenty years the annual imports have varied from a minimum of 68 to a maximum of 94 million dollars a year, on which the duties levied by the tariff have been about 50 per cent. of the declared value. The imports of sugar into the United States are, indeed, only exceeded in their magnitude and value by the imports of wheat into the United Kingdom, in the recent history of international commerce.

In proposing to establish a Trust to regulate the production and price of sugar, it was therefore manifestly to be an organisation that would have to deal with imported as distinguished from indigenous produce, except in so far as the crude imported product might be refined in home refineries.

The New York Senate Committee, which began its investigations into the subject of Trusts in February 1888, examined, among others, a Mr Havemeyer, who described the organisation of the Sugar Trust. He said that the stockholders of various concerns had made an arrangement by which the stockholders of one sugar refining company secured stock in a number of others. The stock was placed in the hands of a board, who issued certificates in return for the interest surrendered. A number of refineries outside the State joined in this arrangement, which was a perpetual one. In reply to the question whether, if he wanted to back out of the Trust, and get back the stock he surrendered, he could do so, he answered that he could not. In surrendering his stock in his own concerns he acquired an interest in all the refineries in the Trust. The profits of all the refineries in the Trust belonged to the certificate holders. It was, therefore, of no consequence to the refineries whether they were running or not. In fact, a number of them had been closed by the board. The aggregate of the certificates issued had been $45,000,000.*

As regards the operation of the Trust or " arrangement " upon the course of production and prices, the witness said that production had not decreased to " any extent." The production of his own refinery, however, had been reduced about one-quarter. The effect of the operations of the Trust upon the market prices of raw and refined sugars had been to render them steady. It had not put up the price of the finished product. It was simply the intention of the board to " prevent the sagging of prices by over-produc-

* This was subsequently increased to 50 million dollars.

tion." The formation of the Trust had not killed competition. Each refinery could sell its own product at its own
prices. The members of the Trust competed and underbid
each other, but "not to the same disastrous extent as
formerly, as they had a good understanding." Through the
operation of the Trust the price of sugar had been less to
the consumer than it had been for five years.

The Sugar Trust took action of a very arbitrary, and, on
the face of it, a very objectionable character with a view
to controlling production. One of the first things that it
did was to order one of the largest refineries in New York—
that of Moller, Sierck & Co.—to be closed, thereby throw-
ing many hands out of employment. Other establishments
absorbed by the Trust were dealt with in a similar way,
including the North River, the Oxward, and the Havemeyer
Companies. The Trust was not able to secure possession
of all the large sugar refineries, and those that remained
independent had, of course, the advantage of the improvement in prices due to the monopolistic operations which it
called into existence. Not only so, but they had advantages exceeding those enjoyed by the members of the Trust,
inasmuch as the stock of the latter was largely watered, so
that a private concern could pay 20 per cent. on its real
capital, when the Trust could only pay 5 per cent. on its
three-quarters inflated stock.

Nor had the Trust a career of unalloyed prosperity in
other directions. The great question of how far the
organisation was legal was raised again and again, and
threatened to jeopardise its existence. These inquiries
bear so directly upon the most fundamental principle involved in the establishment of Trusts, that they may
suitably be referred to.

The first of the cases brought to test the legality of the Sugar Trust was, in January 1889, decided by Judge Barrett, of the New York Supreme Court. The case was brought by the Attorney-General of the State against the North River Sugar Refining Company, to secure a decree for the forfeiture and dissolution of the charter of the company, on the ground that it had exceeded its powers in becoming a member of the Trust. Judge Barrett's decision was against the legality of the Trust. After a review of the provisions of the Trust agreement, and of the testimony elicited in the course of the proceedings, he arrived at the conclusion that the corporations joined in the Trust were a series of corporations transacting business under the forms of law, without real membership or genuinely qualified direction—mere abstract fragments of statutory creation—without life in the concrete or underlying association. The holding of shares of stock transferred by the Trust board to such persons as the board might desire to constitute directors, under the obligation to re-transfer the same when requested, was not, Judge Barrett held, a compliance with the statutory requirement that directors shall be stockholders in their corporations. The Judge, in dealing with the question whether the combination was one of corporations or merely one of stockholders, said that there was a complete practical identity of corporations and stockholders, and that, where the whole body of shareholders offended, the corporation offended. Forfeiture and dissolution followed, he said, as just and legal results. Other proceedings were brought against the Trust in the same year (1889) for conspiracy, on the ground that its members had combined to commit acts injurious to trade or commerce.

The decision of Judge Barrett, by which the charter of

the Sugar Trust was annulled, was afterwards confirmed by
the Supreme Court of the State of New York, which held
that the North River Sugar Refining Company, against
which the prosecution was instituted, had, by transferring
its business and property to the Trust, and thus giving the
management of its affairs to a body of men differing entirely
from that designated by the statute, offended against the
law under which it was created. The Sugar Trust was
stated to have been founded "to secure by substantial
organization, for an indefinite period of time, the control of
the sugar business, and it must be supposed that it was
intended to use that control for the pecuniary benefit of the
associates, and that the direct and usual way in which that
is accomplished is by the advancement of prices of the
commodities manufactured and sold in the way of the business whose control is thus secured." The Court proceeded
to state that "a jury would be justified in concluding from
the Trust agreement and the other evidence in the case,
that the governing object of the association was to promote
its interests and advance the prosperity of the association,
by limiting the supply when that could properly be done,
and advancing the prices of the products produced by the
companies. Where such appeared to be the case, the
association, or arrangement, or whatever else it may be
called, having for its objects the removal of competition
and the advancement of prices of necessaries of life, is
subject to the condemnation of the law, by which it is
denounced as a criminal enterprise. So far as regards the
Trust itself. As regards the particular defendant in the
case, the North River Sugar Refining Company, the Court
held that it had not only entered into an unlawful combination; but had, in so doing, renounced and abandoned its

own duties and subverted its own franchises, thus rendering it liable to the order annulling its charter." So far, then, it will be seen that the judges before whom the case was brought were unanimous in holding the Sugar Trust to be unlawful.

The object of the Sugar Trust, as stated, was to control the production of both refined and raw sugar, thus regulating the general course of prices in the sugar market. The capital of the Trust was 60 millions of dollars (about 12 millions sterling). The owners of the refineries who became parties to the Trust received certificates to the extent of four-fold their value. In other words, they received 400,000 dols. of stock for every 100,000 dols. of actual value. Directly after the Trust was constituted, these certificates were selling in the market at 80 for 100 par.

The Sugar Trust while in its hey-day earned enormous profits. This is proved by the fact that it paid to its shareholders dividends amounting to $10\frac{1}{2}$ % upon its inflated and watered capital of fifty millions of dols.—two-thirds of the capital being taken as "water." The Trust has always been opposed by the Spreckles refineries in San Francisco and Philadelphia, and hence has not been able to raise prices to the level that they would probably otherwise have attained. These refineries, indeed, "have acted as a balance-wheel in regulating the price of refined sugar, which has fluctuated purely in sympathy with the varying relations of supply and demand." *

* Report of New York Chamber of Commerce, 1890-91, part ii. p. 7.

CHAPTER X.

THE COPPER TRUST.

No combination that has been founded within recent years has had a more eventful history, or been so signal a failure, as the combination that was formed in France, some years ago, for the purpose of acquiring the command of the copper supply of the world, and thereby so far limiting production as to create an artificial scarcity of the metal and a consequent increase of its value. The operations of this combination were purely speculative, and they were from every point of view entirely indefensible. The parties who originated the movement were not themselves concerned in the product to be handled, either as consumers or as producers; the operation was a "ring" pure and simple; and it met the fate which all such mischievous enterprises are likely to meet when not founded upon a sufficient justification, or attained by a speculative trick.

The copper ring, which was established in 1887, commenced to buy stocks of copper at about £40 per ton, and they had bought very largely before their movements were generally known. Through their persistence in buying up all the copper in the market, the price of Chili bars was carried to over £100 per ton. But, of course, the ring could not hope to maintain its hold on the market by simply acquiring the floating stocks, since it would have been possible for most of the great copper companies to extend their output, and so to deluge the market, so long as the high prices lasted. One of the first steps taken by the ring was, therefore, to control production, and this they did by making an arrangement with twenty-seven mines or companies to take the whole of their annual output, at a given price, the output of each concern being under regulation. The annual output of these companies was fixed at 175,858 tons, and the total liability incurred by the syndicate was over eleven and a quarter millions sterling. Chili bars, under these circumstances, rose from £44, 5s. in October 1887 to £66, 15s. in November, and £85 in December. During the whole of 1888, as well as in the latter part of 1887, the syndicate must have made immense profits, as the highest price they agreed to pay to producers was £70, and the very large yield of the Calumet and Hecla and Montana Companies was acquired at £61, 10s. per ton.

But the old story of leading the unwilling horse to the water was repeated. Neither the *Société des Métaux* nor the Copper mining companies had reckoned on the fact that the consumers would keep persistently out of the market until prices had fallen. The monthly supplies of copper during a great part of the time that the combination lasted averaged over 10,000 tons, while the consumption fell to about 5000 tons. The supply, therefore, was twice as much as the demand. It became necessary, of course, to do one of two things—either increase the demand or reduce the supply. Neither was easy to the *Société des Métaux*, for they could not bind the public to buy, and they were themselves bound to the copper companies to such an extent that they could not largely reduce the quantities thrown on the market. They had thus got caught on the horns of a

H

dilemma; and either horn was almost as awkward as the other.

The remarkable abstention from purchases that characterised the attitude of buyers is evidenced by the fact that directly the price had fallen the public demand increased, and stocks declined by over 21,000 in about seven months, while the deliveries, which were about 5000 tons per month during the reign of the syndicate, rose to nearly 14,000 tons, so that the price advanced from £38 at the end of April to £48 in November by the reassertion of the law of supply and demand.

In the first week of March 1889, the copper syndicate came to grief, owing to the failure of the French houses to sustain the market, under the pressure of the largely-increased supplies. In the previous three months the visible supply of copper had been increased about 20,000 tons, making the stock in England and France, and the supplies afloat from Chili and Australia to these countries, about 125,000 tons, or about one-half of the then total annual production of copper throughout the world from all sources.

Naturally the immense supplies of copper thus thrown upon the market, brought about the usual consequences of a glut. The price of Chili bars fell from £77, 10s. in January and £78 in February, to £39, 5s. at the end of March. Such a sudden and complete collapse of price had never been known in the trade, and it would have been practically impossible for the strongest corporation to stand against it. The French syndicate held about 120,000 tons of copper when the collapse took place, so that if the fall in price is regarded as so much clear loss, they were likely to drop something like £4,800,000. But the syndicate did not purchase their stocks at the higher figures named. The prices at which they bought varied from £60 to £70 per ton, the greater part of the stock in hand having been secured at an intermediate figure. Of course, when copper dropped to £20 or more below the price at which the *Société* had bought, the road to ruin was clearly marked, and the *facilis descensus Averni* became much accelerated.

The history of the *Société des Metaux* supplies a notable example of the attitude that producers and consumers are likely, under ordinary circumstances, to take in reference to a combination of that character, and of the extremely risky and precarious tenure of that "fearful joy" which speculators so employed are likely to feel. The attitude of the producers is simple and natural enough. They had, to the number of twenty-seven—including all the principal mining companies—the offer of what appeared to be an exceptionally strong financial corporation to take up and dispose of all their produce at a price that left them a much larger margin of profit than they were then able to secure under a free fighting trade. Although copper is a notoriously speculative metal, it has not often been so high in price as £60 a ton. The producers, therefore, were likely to seize with avidity the opportunity of disposing of the whole of their produce at prices not otherwise obtainable, even if that compact involved a reduction of make and deliveries. While the game lasted, it suited the copper companies admirably.

When the *Comptoir d'Escompte* liquidated, as a result of the failure of the *Société des Metaux*, it had advanced over 100 million francs on the security of copper owned by the syndicate, on a basis of over £40 per ton. It had guaranteed contracts, having two years to run, with copper producing concerns of the magnitude of the Rio Tinto Company. Finally it had agreed to take about 80,000 tons of copper, if the syndicate did not do so, at £60 per ton.   In short, the whole capital and reserves of the second financial institution of France were embarked in a most hazardous speculation, and that its depositors, whose claims amounted to over four millions sterling, suffered no loss was due to the advance of that, and an additional sum, by the Bank of France.   A national calamity was thus averted, but it was at the cost of forcing the institution which officially represents the government, to take over the questionable assets of a ruined bank.   Such a shock to confidence, in a country so peculiarly sensitive to such impressions as France, was naturally of a most destructive type.

Next to the subversive effect on the whole banking system of the country, came the positive losses in the wiping out or depreciation of securities.   The capital and reserve of the *Comptoir d'Escompte* amounted to 100,000,000 francs. Its 500 franc shares sold not long before at 1000 francs each. They now sold below 100 francs each.   The *Société des Metaux*, the formal organization of the syndicate, had a capital of nearly 60,000,000 francs.   Its shares sold at one time at 1,200 francs each.   Their price now fell to about 25 francs.   The Rio Tinto mines, in which the chief auxiliary share speculation of the syndicate was conducted, were largely owned in Paris.   The market value of their shares fell from 500 francs to about half of that amount. In short, a loss from shrinkages mounting up towards 150,000,000 francs was seen in the securities directly involved in the downfall of the copper syndicate.

Other interests are said to have suffered correspondingly. Paris is a great speculative and investment market.   It is the seat of great financial institutions, and on the Bourse many classes of government securities, and shares of rail-road, commercial, and industrial enterprises are dealt in. All of these had to endure a shrinkage. Altogether a more pitiable story of failure and disaster has seldom had to be told, and its only redeeming feature is the reflection that a defeat so overwhelming is likely to stand as a beacon-light to warn others from similarly sinister operations, if they would avoid a similarly crushing retribution.

CHAPTER XI.

THE BRITISH CHEMICAL TRUST.

DURING the last thirty years no industry has grown with more rapid strides than that which is known as the chemical manufacture, and the principal products of which are soda and bleaching powder. The Tyne, the Tees, the Mersey, and other industrial rivers of Great Britain, bear testimony, which many will probably regard as only too obvious, to the extent and variety of this manufacture. The chemical trade is, however, not only subject to considerable vicissitudes from the usual ups and downs of the market, but it has all along been peculiarly liable to changes of a more or less revolutionary character from within, induced by the invention and adoption of new processes of manufacture, founded upon new chemical reactions and discoveries. Hence it has happened that the works in one district would be extremely successful in consequence of adopting a more economical process, while those of another district would be in adverse circumstances from their inability to compete with the newest applications of chemical science, which they were probably not in a position to apply at the moment.

It was in these circumstances that the idea was conceived, in the latter part of the year 1890, of founding a chemical union or syndicate, intended to embrace all the different establishments employed in the soda or alkali industry.

The ammonia process of manufacturing soda had then come well to the front, and the makers of that product by the old Le Blanc method found it difficult to compete with the newer system. The extent to which the new method was an improvement upon the old is pretty clearly evidenced by the fact that while in the first half of the year 1890 one establishment engaged in the new ammonia process had made a profit of over £89,000, and a well-known establishment on the Tyne, which continued to follow the Le Blanc method, incurred a loss of £20,000 in the sale of their soda ash. The manufacturers who followed the old Le Blanc process admitted the superiority of the alkali manufactured under the ammonia or Solvay process, but they found it difficult and inexpedient to make an immediate change. The well known chemical works of Allhusen & Co., on the Tyne, were specially constructed for the production of soda by the Le Blanc system, and for many years they found this to be an extremely profitable business. When Mr Solvay appeared upon the scene with his ammonia process,* he certainly produced carbonate of soda of greater purity than that yielded by the Le Blanc method, but he allowed the chlorine which formed the greater part of the raw material—common salt or brine—to go to waste, whereas in the Le Blanc process the chlorine is utilised for the production of bleaching powder, or chloride of lime. The fact determined the Newcastle Chemical Co. and other companies to stick to the Le Blanc process—at least for a time—the determining consideration having been thus ex-

---

* This process is based upon a well-known chemical reaction, which permits of the production of soda by means of carbonic acid acting upon ammonia and brine.

pressed by Mr Christian Allhusen at a meeting of the company held in 1890 :—

"Civilised man requires chlorine just as material man requires bread ; and the fact that we can produce chlorine as cheaply as any firm or company in the world, is the sole excuse for the determined struggle we have carried on, and are now carrying on, for the continuance of our existence."

The distressed condition of the alkali works carrying on the Le Blanc process, was the immediate and most urgent *raison d'être* for the establishment, in the autumn of 1890, of the Chemical Union—an organisation which embraced most of the leading firms of alkali manufacturers throughout the United Kingdom. This, however, was not by any means the first organisation of its kind in the country. For many years a similar association was carried on among the manufacturers of bleaching powder with the object of controlling production. This association came to grief at the end of 1889, and as efforts made to bring about its re-establishment proved ineffectual, and as the production of bleaching powder thereupon was largely increased, the price of that commodity rapidly fell, and in a few months was £2 per ton under that which prevailed while the association was in existence. This was, of course, a serious blow to the manufacturers of soda by the Le Blanc system, because they were the principal producers of bleaching powder, and had extended the means of production, as admitted by the chairman of the Newcastle Chemical Company, far beyond the actual requirements of bleachers and paper manufacturers. These firms were thus face to face with a double trouble—they were unable to compete with the Solvay process as alkali makers, and the bleaching powder, on which they depended for their profits, had become a drug in the market, and had fallen to an unremunerative range of prices.

When the Union or Trust was constituted in 1890 for the purpose of carrying on the alkali works of the United Kingdom as one industrial enterprise, it was stated that most of the works which it was proposed to acquire had been carried on at a profit. No doubt this was quite true as regards the ammonia process works, but it was not equally true in reference to most of the others, which, for the reasons already stated, were more or less *in extremis*, so that the good concerns had literally to bear the burden of the bad ones. This is an inevitable condition of forming syndicates of the kind in any industry. If the production or price is to be regulated, the whole of the works likely to be benefited, or likely to compete, must be taken into account, whether they are successful or unsuccessful, prosperous or the reverse. This is simply another way of saying that the strong works or firms are much less likely to gain anything from a regulated price than those that are weak and needy. The result is that it is generally the weak and impecunious works that are most anxious to establish a syndicate, and it was so in the case of the Alkali Union, although the larger and stronger firms also to a larger extent became parties to the agreement.

One effect of the establishment of the Chemical Union was to give a great impetus to the production of chemical wood pulps. This system of producing fibre for the manufacture of paper does not call for the use of soda, the fibre required being produced by simply boiling in sulphurous acid. Nor does chemical wood pulp call for the use of bleaching powder, like ordinary materials, except for paper of the very highest class. Hence, it is clear that when soda and bleaching powder were largely raised in price by an artificial combination, it became the interest of the paper manufacturers, who are among the best customers of the alkali trade, to become as far as possible independent of the use of chemicals at prohibitive prices, and this they did by encouraging the use of wood pulp, not previously adopted on a very large scale. Large works for the production of this pulp were erected in Germany, Austria, the United States, and other countries, and the output was speedily increased by thousands of tons. Orders were, of course, withdrawn to a corresponding extent from the manufacturers of alkali and bleaching powder, by whatever process produced, so that the good and successful works suffered equally with those that were bad and unsuccessful.

Another result that followed upon the establishment of the Chemical Union was, that papermakers and other manufacturers who still required to consume the chemicals affected, began to make arrangements for erecting works to supply their own demands. "We cannot," they said in effect, "afford to have our markets taken from us for our own products by foreign competitors, the price of whose chemicals is not kept up by artificial means like our own." This matter did, indeed, receive a good deal of attention from the committee of the Chemical Union, and from the manufacturers that consumed the chemicals. The former declared that the consumers could not produce their chemicals so cheaply as the Union was prepared to supply them, while the latter contended that they could easily produce more cheaply than the Union, because they could rely on providing works which would, of course, be equipped with all the most modern appliances for economical production.

The Chemical Union has, since its establishment, been conducted with a reasonable amount of prudence. No attempt has been made to extort exorbitant prices from consumers. The price of bleaching powder has been pretty evenly maintained, but it has not been higher than it was during the six years preceding the establishment of the Union, during which time, however, prices were artificially increased, as stated, by the operations of the Bleaching Powder Association.

CHAPTER XII.

On the first blush, it might appear as if it were all but impossible to successfully establish a monopoly in an industry that is followed on such an enormous scale, and is of such world-wide extent, as that of shipping. No nation that has any pretensions to civilisation is without the means to a larger or a less extent, of breaking down, as far as its own commerce is concerned, an operation of this kind. And yet the fact remains, that monopolies have been established in the shipping business, and that, too, within comparatively recent years.

This circumstance is one of such serious and general import in relation to the business of the world, that it demands an unusually close and careful consideration. If shipping business can be brought under monopolist influence, and if any body of men, as companies, however powerful and wealthy, have it in their power to either prejudice the interests of those outside the combination in their own trade, or the general interests of the public in so far as they are capable of being affected by the monopoly, it should be much more easy to bring about the results in industries whose operations are carried on within a more limited area, and less exposed to outside competition.

When the question of the existence of a ring in the Australian shipping trade was recently under discussion, it was generally believed that the organisation was one of all the leading firms engaged in this trade to refuse freights that did not come up to a certain sum, so that the freighter who failed to comply with the terms proposed would find himself unable to get his goods shipped at all.

As a matter of fact, the ring was not one of shipowners at all, but of the class called loading brokers. The business of the loading broker is to pay a lump sum for the whole cargo space of a ship for a given voyage, and let out this space in small quantities to the various merchants who have goods to ship. In other words, he buys cargo space wholesale and sells it retail, as one might buy and sell any commodity in general use. The Australian freight ring was simply an association of loading brokers, who agreed among themselves not to retail the cargo space in ships bound to Australia at less than a given rate. The brokers who were parties to this arrangement never, at any time, succeeded in monopolising the whole of the ships in the Australian trade. Indeed, when the ring was wielding the greatest amount of power, about the end of 1887, and when the so-called "nefarious" character of its business was most loudly complained of, there were other vessels loading in London against it. Many important firms had, however, signed agreements which bound them to ship all their goods from London to Australia by the ships belonging to the ring, and those who entered into such covenants were, of course, unable to take advantage of the fluctuations of freight rates that took place when ships were put on in opposition to the ring, and caused rates to drop suddenly from 20s. to 10s. and even 7s. per ton. For this inability to buy freight space in the cheapest market, the shippers had, of course themselves to blame. They were in the position of a coal-owner who has made a contract to pay a certain royalty per ton of coal raised at a time when the price of coal is high, and who is thereby prevented from taking advantage of the cheaper royalty rents awarded to his neighbour when coal is selling at a low price, and is a drug in the market.

One of the largest shipping firms in the iron trade wrote to *The Times* to complain of the arbitrary manner in which the shipping ring exercised its powers. Messrs Lysaght & Co. of Bristol had contracted to sign an agreement with the Australian brokers under which they were compelled to ship all goods intended for the Antipodes, not from Bristol, but from London. Meanwhile another firm, acting in opposition to the ring, put on opposition ships, and offered to take Messrs Lysaght's goods at a through rate from Bristol to Sydney and Melbourne. This, of course, was a great advantage to the shippers, who had not, under the terms proposed, to incur the cost of sending their goods to London for shipment, and not unnaturally they accepted the offer. But as the Australian ring deemed this to be a contravention of the agreement made with them, the agreement was cancelled, and the members of the ring refused to ship any more goods for Messrs Lysaght unless at a prohibitive price. Messrs Lysaght offered to submit the matter in dispute to arbitration, but the offer was declined, and the consequence was that the freighters had to submit to the dictation of the ring or combine with others to suppress it, and it need hardly be added that the latter alternative was one that was not easy to carry into effect.

It will, of course, be asked why should freighters put themselves into the hands of a shipping combination of this character with their eyes open, and thereby deprive themselves of the opportunity of taking advantage of the best

terms likely to be available? The answer is simple. It
was done under compulsion. The ring required all Australian merchants and shipping agents to sign an agreement by
which they were precluded from shipping by any sailing
ship loading for Australian ports other than those loaded
by members of the ring, on pain of having an extra rate of
freight charged. No important shipper could afford to be
thus practically placed at a disadvantage in competition
with others in the same trade. It was like putting a loaded
pistol at the head of the shippers. The brokers had, of
course made for themselves a very strong position before
they could afford to take such a high-handed step. They
boasted, indeed, that they had accumulated from surplus
profits a sum of £80,000, wherewith to fight all opposition,
and the moment that opposition, in the form of lower rates
of freight, was offered, the brokers found it worth their while
to underbid the lowest rates that were possible, and even
to undertake freights that could not fail to be attended with
absolute loss.

From the brokers' point of view, it need hardly be said
that they had a great interest at stake. So long as they
were able to keep their ring going they were enabled to
keep themselves quite free from competition, alike as
regards their dealings with the shipowner—from whom, in
most cases, they chartered the ships that they employed—
and with the merchant, who was left without choice, no
matter how unsatisfactory the arrangement might be on
economic grounds. Strangely enough, the brokers were
enabled, so long as their combination lasted, to dominate
both shipowners and merchants, in consequence of the conditions under which the Australian trade was carried on.
The shipowner who wanted to charter his ship for an

Australian voyage had to apply to one of the ring, and the members of the combination settled among themselves what rate they should give. From this rate the shipowner had practically no appeal, unless he was prepared to strike out an absolutely new line for himself, and this, of course, was attended with much trouble and uncertainty. Besides, the ring generally offered the shipowner what was considered reasonable terms, and certainly better terms than he could have commanded, in a general way, had he had the temerity to work against them. The merchant, on the other hand, was compelled to come to the brokers for a rate of freight, since the ships in the Australian trade were practically entirely at their disposal, and the combination not only settled the rate that must be paid, but they fixed the time at which, and the vessel by which, the goods were to be shipped.

The freight ring had, of course, to encounter the competition of continental ports, and it may at once be asked why did not the shippers of English goods ship from Antwerp or Hamburg? The answer to this is that it has been found politic for a freight ring to prevent continental opposition by clearing the continental ports of their better class goods, which are usually carried at high rates of freight, by booking them through *viâ* London at a greatly reduced rate, or, if there is sufficient, by sending an occasional vessel to the continental port to take them in there. One well authenticated case is cited of continental fine goods, shipped from Hamburg *viâ* London to Australia by P. and O. steamer at a through rate of 50s. per ton to cover everything, while English goods by the same steamer were charged 60s. from the London docks, and shippers had to deliver alongside at the docks, at a considerable additional cost for cartage, dock dues, &c.   In such a case, of course, the continental manufacturer is enabled to sell at an advantage which is fatal to his English competitor, and it is beyond all question that freight rings have driven many classes of bulky goods from England into Continental channels, while the measures which such combinations have adopted, in order to prevent the development of the direct carrying trade from Continental ports, are equivalent to the payment of a considerable premium upon the better class of goods to the continental manufacturers.   So far, indeed, has this been carried that some manufacturers have declared that the influence of freight rings upon the industries in which they were engaged, would be sufficient, if their property in England were of a realizable character, to make it profitable for them to transfer their capital to the Continent, and to pursue their business there.   Instances in proof of this statement have been actually furnished in the cases of the wire, the cement, and the bottled beer trades.   The large Australian demand for these three articles has, it is said, been supplied by Continental factories to a large extent from Hamburg, Antwerp, and other Continental ports, because the high rates of freight from England have been fatal to the competition of English manufacturers.

In the case of freight rings an element comes into play that is hardly found to operate in the case of ordinary industrial syndicates.   The shipping trade is one that enjoys in a special, and generally unique, degree the advantage of bounties and subsidies.   In our own country, subsidies are paid to such lines as the P. and O. for carrying the mails.   On the Continent bounties are paid both for the building and the working of ships.   The German Government some years ago heavily subsidised a

I

line of steamers, intended to load from Hamburg and Flushing, for the express purpose of assisting German manufacturers to develop their direct trade with the Australasian colonies.   At the same time, the British Government was making large grants of public money to an English line whose policy, in so far as they were parties to the shipping ring, was absolutely fatal to the success of British trade.   It has been suggested that in making such grants in the future to the leading shipping lines, Government should attach a condition that the grant should be liable to forfeiture if it were proved that the company had either joined a ring or boycotted a shipper.   So far as the facts are known this condition should not be difficult to carry out, but it does not always happen that the true facts come to the knowledge of those who have the power to apply the remedy. The parties to the contracts and arrangements made with the object of controlling prices or freights have usually something "up their sleeve," which only comes to light when the State has ordered a committee or a commission to inquire into the whole matter.

The specific question involved in the case of the Mogul Shipping Company was that of the legality of a combination between a number of ship-owners and transportation companies which, with a view to securing exclusive control of the tea-carrying trade from Hankow and Shanghai to London, allowed a rebate of 5 per cent. on the freight to firms which shipped by other than combination vessels. One company, which had been for some time admitted to the combination or conference, was afterwards excluded therefrom, the China merchants being warned by a circular that anyone shipping in the vessels of that company would lose the rebate.   The company sought to gain a portion of the trade by cutting rates, but the combination lowered its rates in turn, and the excluded company lost its freights. It thereupon brought a suit against the members of the combination on the ground that the combination amounted to an unlawful conspiracy to deprive it of its share of the trade.

This case was tried, in the first instance, before Lord Chief-Justice Coleridge, who gave judgment for the defendants. He held that the combination among the defendants to secure the trade in question to themselves was not illegal, but came within the bounds of legitimate trade competition. The defendants had, he said, the right to offer inducements to customers to deal exclusively with them, by giving them notice that only exclusive customers would have these exceptional advantages. He saw in the circumstances of the case nothing upon which to base a charge of coercion or bribery, and nothing to show that the combination was one in restraint of trade in the legal sense. This decision of Lord Chief-Justice Coleridge was affirmed in July 1889 by a majority of the Court of Appeal, who held, in substance, that as the combination of the defendants was simply in order to promote their own gain, there was nothing illegal in it, provided the members did not circulate false rumours, or resort to intimidation or fraud, in order to destroy the competition of the plaintiff.

CHAPTER XIII.

THE AMERICAN WHISKY AND OTHER TRUSTS.

THE extent to which the movement for the establishment of trusts in the United States has proceeded has been indicated in a previous section. One of the large products that came under treatment as a trust business was whisky. This Trust had an eventful history, and presents some features that are deserving of special consideration.

The Whisky Trust was founded in the year 1887. The trade is a strong one, and the Trust found little difficulty in providing a large fund for the purpose of fighting its rivals in other parts of the country who had not come within its ample folds. One of its first movements was to drop the price of whisky to such a low point, that the non-syndicated producers could not compete with the Trust without incurring a heavy loss. In this way two objects were to be gained. The Trust was likely, in the first place, to secure a reputation for benefiting consumers, instead of incurring the reproach of raising the price of the commodity, and on the other hand, it was expected that the low price at which the Trust was prepared to sell would kill off some of the weaker competitors.

The reign of low prices was not, however, of long duration. With occasional advances, attributed to the rise in the price of corn, the Trust did not venture on a high range of prices until June 1890, when a considerable increase in the price of corn brought about a material advance in the price of alcohol. Professor Jenks has, however, pointed out that while an increase in the price of alcohol was necessary to meet the increase in the price of corn, a much greater advance was made than was required to strike a balance; * and figures which he compiled showed that, whereas the advance in the price of corn justified an increase of five cents per gallon in the price of whisky, the actual advance made by the Trust was not less than twelve cents per gallon.

With such a material advance in the selling price of the product, the American Whisky Trust was able to declare greatly improved dividends, as compared with the individual distillers. Professor Jenks states † that "the Whisky Trust has regularly declared dividends of from one-eighth to one-half per cent. per month since its organisation," and that when the surplus is taken into account, "this has probably made for them an earning of at least 12 per cent. a year, during the latter period, on the capital invested, and perhaps 15 or 18 per cent., as the testimony of some of its members showed that the value of the plant was about one-third of the nominal value of the stock."

Before the establishment of the Whisky Trust there had been several combinations of distillers in the United States, designed to take measures against over-production. At one time such an organisation limited the production to 28 per cent., and at another time to 40 per cent. of the normal capacity of the distilleries. About the time when the Civil War was begun, the Government of the United States largely raised the excise tax on whisky, at first to twenty cents,

* The *Economic Journal*, March 1892, p. 89.
† *Ibid.*, p. 94.

and finally to two dollars per gallon, allowing a considerable interval to intervene before the higher rate was levied. This offered a great stimulus to the trade, and is said to have called into existence many more distilleries than would have been built under normal conditions, so that the business has generally suffered from the evils of over-production in an unusual degree. After the formation of the Whisky Trust, it was found that twelve distilleries, running to the full extent of their capacity, produced as much as eighty distilleries had produced previously. Of course, these eighty distilleries had to produce quantities much under their capacity, and profits would be likely to be correspondingly reduced.

The Brewery Trust.—Some years ago—in April 1889— there was some talk of establishing a great Brewery Trust in the United States, with a view to regulating the production and the price of beer. There were then stated to be two thousand breweries in America, with an annual production of over twenty-five millions of barrels, and this industry was said to employ more capital than any other in the United States (flour alone excepted) engaged in the production of food staples. The extent and wide scope of the beer industry rendered it difficult to establish a trust of the character suggested, but a syndicate was formed for the purpose of endeavouring, if not to establish a trust, at any rate to secure options on the principal properties of this description, in order to make money "by floating the stocks on the London Stock Exchange." The result was conspicuous in the new issues for 1889-90. But there has for some years been a protective pool among the brewers of New York City, which regulates prices, discounts, and terms, and has, it is said, proved very advantageous to the trade. This was a case where the public voice would probably pronounce a trust to be excusable if not beneficial, as in the case of the Whisky Trust, provided, of course, that prices were raised so high as to keep down the consumption.

The Milk Exchange, Limited, was a combination established in the city of New York, which, though not exactly a trust in the ordinary and usual acceptation of the term, was an organisation which was established for the purpose of destroying competition, and it has been denounced by the General Laws Committee of the Senate of New York State as "a monopoly of the worst sort." This Corporation was formed with the ostensible object of buying and selling milk. It has been exclusively a middleman's organisation, and it has been complained that they, through its authority, fix the price of milk. In brief, the farmer is obliged, in consequence of the large extent of the ramifications of the Milk Exchange, to sell his milk to that corporation at two and three cents a quart, while the Exchange is left free to charge consumers in the city seven or eight cents, and at times as much as ten cents a quart, in their discretion. The Senate Committee recommended in 1888 that owing to such proceedings the Charter of the Company should be forfeited, but, after all, it is doubtful whether the Milk Exchange does more or worse things than are done every day by individuals and companies that have the command of a large capital, and are in a position to fix prices over a large area.

The Salt Trust.—In the English salt industry there had been reckless competition, and an undercutting of prices for many years prior to 1889. The average price of salt, which not so many years ago had been as much as 20s. per ton, had gradually fallen until during the ten years ending

1889, the highest price of salt at the mines or works was 7s., and many thousands of tons were sold as low as 2s. 6d. The competition was strong enough while Cheshire and Worcestershire had the business practically entirely in their own hands, but when the Cleveland district came into the field it grew keener still.   To put an end to this futile competition, and consolidate the interests of the various owners of salt mines and works, a Salt Union or Syndicate was established in 1889, which ultimately included every salt proprietor of any position in the country.   Since then, the Union has paid much better average dividends than the salt-owners could have paid individually, and that, too, without raising the price of salt to ordinary consumers to an extent that can be materially felt.   Large consumers of salt, like the alkali manufacturers, have, of course, felt the pinch more keenly.

Steel Rail Trusts.—There are probably few commodities that so readily lend themselves to the regulation of production and of price on a large scale as steel rails.   The manufacture of railway material is in comparatively few hands, whether in England or abroad.   There are not more than eight or ten firms engaged in this industry in Great Britain, and probably there are not so many in Germany. It is much the same in the United States, where the trade is chiefly concentrated in the hands of two large companies —the Carnegie Company at Pittsburgh, and the Illinois Steel Company at Chicago.   The manufacture and sale of steel rails has consequently been more or less regulated for a very considerable time.   The most important organisation of this description was formed in London in 1883, and flourished for something like three years, one of its more prominent features being that it had, up to a certain point, an international character, in so far as it included German and Belgian manufacturers.*

German Coal Trusts.—Attempts have been made to regulate the production and price of coal in the Dortmund coal-field at several periods since the year 1879, when a crisis of unusual severity led to the establishment of one of the first syndicates founded for that purpose. M. Gruner, who has made a special study of these syndicates,† remarks that the original agreement, which was mainly intended to limit production, was made only for a year, and at the end of each succeeding twelve months its terms were greatly modified. One of the conditions imposed on the coal-owners who became parties to the agreement was that, if they exceeded the limit of production fixed by the syndicate they should incur certain monetary penalties, which were applied to the provident and benefit organisations carried on for the benefit of the miners. This penalty was usually more or less according to the excess of production, and varied from a minimum of 6d. to a maximum of 2s. per ton of overplus.

The syndicate had, however, a very chequered and stormy career. Great difficulty was found in fixing from year to year the quantity of coal to be produced from each mine. In 1884, thirty-eight of the principal mines withdrew from the organisation, and although the penalty fixed for exceeding the production agreed upon was the considerable one of 2s. per ton, several concerns, tempted by comparatively high prices, exceeded largely the prescribed limits,

* The history and working of this organisation were described by its President in his evidence before the Royal Commission on the Depression of Trade, December 17th, 1885.

† *Les Associations et Syndicats Miniers en Allemagne.*

so that the total output of 1885, instead of being 8½ per cent. under that of the previous year, was actually 2 per cent. above it.   On these facts, M. Gruner remarks :—

"Les résultats obtenus par le syndicat pour la réduction de la production furent donc presque nuls : d'une part, les exceptions qui avaient dû être consenties pour satisfaire aux exigences de certains membres, ôtaient beaucoup de leur efficacité aux clauses de réduction ; d'autre part, la pénalité convenue n'était pas un obstacle au développement de production de certains associés situés dans des conditions économiques spécialement avantageuses.

"Ainsi, pour ne citer qu'un exemple, une compagnie qui avait cependant adhéré au syndicat, avait produit, en 1886, 76.206 tonnes de plus que ne le permettait la convention ; elle fut donc tenue, de ce chef, à verser à la caisse syndicale une somme de 188,015 francs.   Elle avait trouvé avantage à subir cette amende plutôt que de réduire sa production, estimant que cette cotisation n'augmentait que de 6 centimes son prix de revient et que l'augmentation résultant d'une réduction de production eût été notablement plus considérable.

"C'est en vain qu'on chercha de nouvelles bases pour asseoir une nouvelle convention, à prendre cours le 1er janvier 1887 ; tous les efforts demeurèrent infructueux.

"En présence de cet insuccès, la majorité des intéressés songea alors à imposer légalement ses volontés par l'intermédiaire de la Caisse des mines, à laquelle toutes les mines de la circonscription sont obligatoirement affiliées."

For several years following the failure of the Dortmund Coal Syndicate, the coal industry of that district was in a very unsatisfactory condition.   Prices fell almost continuously, and returns were published which showed that the average dividends paid by the principal companies over a series of years, did not exceed 3 per cent. In June 1887, accordingly, Dr Hammacher, President of the Association for the Defence of Mining Interests at Dortmund, proposed the establishment of an association for the pooling of the coal supply of Westphalia, so far as the principal collieries were concerned, following the system already adopted in the case of the coke manufacture of the same locality.

In this latter case, a Coke Manufacturers' Association was founded in the year 1885, and for a period of fifteen months it was carried on successfully, and succeeded in maintaining prices; but owing to the withdrawal of some 30 per cent. of the producers, who preferred to be independent, the association was dissolved in October 1886. At a later date the syndicate was re-established on more satisfactory lines, and succeeded in securing the cohesion of 99 per cent. of the total output of coke in Westphalia. The disposal of the output is controlled by a committee, who fix the quantities to be produced, and the price has been kept up with a fair amount of success while the syndicate has been in existence.

CHAPTER XIV.

THE relations of the railways of different countries to the public interests have often been marked by combinations to keep up particular rates, or conditions, which may be variously regarded as a pool, a trust, or a ring (according to its circumstances) of a different form. In the United States, railways have no protection or monopoly beyond what they can create for themselves by sheer strength and endurance. Any one can build a railroad wherever he likes, and when a competing line is threatened, the already established lines do not, as in Great Britain, rush to Parliament to seek for statutory powers to keep out the threatened intruder, or rather to have such powers refused to the newcomer. Each railway company or corporation must fight, like "Hal o' the Wynd," for "his ain han'." Competition has thus been made much keener and more general in America than in Great Britain, France, or Germany, where a particular company has usually a monopoly of a particular district.

The usual process adopted by the established railway interest is to retain possession of the traffic, and starve out its competitor by cutting rates. This process may or may not be one of natural selection, but it is certainly one which, if it were sufficiently long-continued, would compel the weakest to go to the wall. The practically unrestricted liberty to build railroads enjoyed in the United States, is a principal element in the instability and fluctuations of American railway property.   No line is exempt from the danger of having to share a certain portion of what appears to be a practically monopolist traffic with some new-comer, and if the ultimate result should happen, as is very likely, to be bad for the new-comer, it is certainly not good for the established concern.   A cut-throat competition to-day is probably followed by a pooling or dividing arrangement to-morrow, and a cutting of rates again the day after.

Combinations are also common between different railway concerns, for the purpose of securing a share of through traffic, and, if possible, diverting such traffic from other lines. This form of combination has not, as a rule, been adverse to the public interest.   On the contrary, through, or competitive, rates have in general been greatly reduced, and in many cases to such an extent as to cause discrimination against local or non-competitive traffic.   Such combinations to procure through traffic have been carried so far, in the United States at anyrate, that no important line is now worked independently of its connections.

Such combinations, again, usually aim at four different results, namely (1) to secure all the traffic possible ; (2) to secure such traffic for the longest possible haul ; (3) to convey as much traffic as possible to the markets of the commercial centres, upon the prosperity of which that of the road mainly depends ; and (4) to obtain the best paying rate attainable under all the conditions governing competition between rival markets, and between rival transportation lines.

In order to avoid the great losses that inevitably attend on wars of rates, the Railway Companies of the United

States have, at different times, entered into what are known as pooling arrangements for the apportionment or division of traffic. These arrangements, though they appear to be dictated by reasons of policy, have not been always, or, indeed, generally made without difficulty. In the cutting of rates it was found that each competitor possessed a capacity to injure its rivals exceeding its ability to benefit itself—that the decline of rates involved in such a struggle was not compensated by any possible increase of traffic. Attempts were made, but without success, to secure the intervention of the State, or Federal authority, in deciding matters connected with competitive inter-State traffic, and it was finally left to the various companies concerned to frame regulations for themselves.

The line upon which pooling agreements are framed are in some respects singular. The circumstance that mainly determines the question of what amount of traffic shall be apportioned to each road is the relative ability of each of the several lines concerned to secure traffic for itself. The cost of the transportation of the traffic to each road carrying it, the relation of the receipts to the expenses of each line, and the comparative and relative costs of constructing the several lines that are concerned in the pool, are regarded as minor matters. In some cases the apportionment of the traffic is based upon the tonnage moved, which is called a physical pool; and in other cases the receipts are divided, which is known as a money pool. In some cases the officers of each company keep a record of the amount of traffic actually carried by each line; and in others, the companies having first agreed upon the share of the competitive traffic which each road shall be allowed to have, an agreement is made with the principal freighters that they shall so direct their shipments or freight that each road shall receive the proportion of the competitive.traffic agreed upon.

Numerous pooling arrangements were made on these and similar lines between the principal railways of the United States up to a comparatively recent date. The history and progress of some of the principal pools of this description are set forth in the valuable " Reports on the Internal Commerce of the United States," published by the Treasury office at Washington, so that we need not enter into the subject here at greater length. It may, however, be remarked that railroad pools are usually regarded by the public with much disfavour, and that they have frequently come under the animadversion of the courts of law.

Under the Inter-State Commerce Law of 1886, railways were prohibited from making pooling arrangements. This provision has, however, been subjected to a great deal of adverse criticism. It has been held by a high railway authority that " the prohibition of pooling encourages secret rate-cutting, and leaves the honest and the careful carriers helpless against the dishonest and the reckless." Another has contended that " the provision of the inter-State law, which prohibits railway companies from assisting each other to maintain living rates, while their earnings are constantly being reduced by hostile legislation, is repugnant to the ordinary principles of equity, and threatens general railway bankruptcy." It has been suggested that the object to be accomplished by legalising pools can be attained by enacting " that the highest rate that shall be allowed to be charged in any one year shall be the lowest rate that shall have been charged during the preceding year," and whatever else may be said about such a proposal, it would at least be likely to prevent irresponsible freight agents from involving their companies in freight wars, and business men in large losses. Although under the law named the companies are prevented from making pooling arrangements in the same open way that they did before the law was passed, it is stated that such arrangements are still continued, veiled under private and unwritten understandings which it is difficult to trace.

The establishment of combinations has to a certain extent been restrained, especially in the case of railroads, by the fear of the consequences of resistance on the part of the public. That resistance might conceivably take, and has in reality taken, many different forms. But in so far as it applies to combinations to keep up railway rates, its action would most probably assume the form apprehended by the President of one of the American trunk lines, when, in discussing the so-called "Saratoga compact"—a proposed agreement as to the differences of rates which should prevail between the four principal Atlantic seaports and the principal commercial centres of the Western and North-Western States—he declared that "such a combination would be regarded by the people as being against their interests; that as a result a combination of the people would be formed against the railroads of the country; and that through the courts, the legislatures, and the national congress, hostile action would be induced, which would more than counterbalance the advantages realised from the increased rates that might be commanded through so powerful an organisation." *

The commercial press of the United States, equally with the railway interest, has denounced the absolute prohibi-

* Report on the Internal Commerce of the United States for 1879, p. 161.

tion of pools contained in the Inter-State Commerce Law, and has argued that although there are no doubt abuses connected with the pooling system, the remedy for them is to be found, not in the prohibition of such arrangements, but in their recognition and regulation.* In support of this argument, it is pointed out that in Europe the chief States have come to regard railway pools as a necessity. In Belgium, the Government railways are stated to enter into pooling arrangements with the private roads. In England, arrangements are made between the different railways which practically amount to pooling, as, for example, where they agree upon the rates to be charged to competitive points, and when one company agrees to pay to another a certain annual subsidy in lieu of its share of actual or possible traffic. More or less modified pooling arrangements are common in other European countries, and indeed they are deemed to be essential to the carrying on of railway operations.

A "pool" between different railway companies does not necessarily imply the absence of competition, nor does it in all cases mean that higher rates are to be maintained. On the contrary, there is always to be found the keenest competition, even between lines that pool their traffic, in the effort to secure traffic by special facilities and inducements. On this subject a recent writer has observed :—

"But the interest of the public in the methods of transportation companies is not confined to rates. From the nature of the case competition in facilities is as inevitable as competition in rates is impossible. Railroads differ from stores in this respect. Buyers of merchandise want the largest possible stock to select from, and the lowest possible

* "*Bradstreet's*," December 18th, 1886.

K

prices, and they care much less than is commonly supposed whether they find the cheapest and best goods in a brown stone front or a wooden one. But the traveller who sets out from New York for Chicago, other things being equal, takes the route which gives him the quickest time, the most desirable cars, the most courteous attendance, and the best provision for meals *en route;* while the shipper of freight, other things being equal, chooses the line which experience, or common repute, indicates as most likely to afford prompt dispatch with ample conveniences for loading and discharging. In all these respects, in freight and passenger service alike, every road, so long as it does business at all, must compete with its neighbours. In the matter of rates, the Pennsylvania no more competes with the New York Central than if it had no existence, but in the matter of facilities there is constant and active competition. Competition in facilities is in every way desirable from the standpoint of the public. The more there is of it the better for the community, and probably in the long run for the owners of the railways as well.

" This leads to the question whether the form that railroad combinations take is a matter of indifference. Four possible forms substantially cover the ground. Parallel roads may consolidate, join in an agreement to maintain rates, pool their competitive traffic, or pool their earnings. The 'traffic contracts,' which have become so prominent of late, are in principle only a modified form of pooling. Most railroad men, and some economists, hold that it was a mistake for Congress to prohibit pooling. So far as the rate question is concerned, they are doubtless right. Tariffs are much more easily maintained by pools than by mere agreements upon certain rates. As a rule, pledges to observe good faith and stick to the tariff are made publicly only to be broken secretly, unless the motive for breaking them is taken away. Pools certainly take away this motive. But do they not at the same time take away the motive for enlarging and improving the service given to the public? Agreed rates leave the various companies free to increase their revenues to the utmost."

Another American economist—Professor Hadley—whose well-known book on Railroad Transportation is one of the best of its kind, is of opinion that the countries where pooling is carried to the fullest extent are those in which the evils of discrimination are best avoided, and he even goes the length of affirming that the worst forms of discrimination can be avoided only by a system of pooling.

But whether Congress was right or wrong in its prohibition of railway pooling arrangements, there is no doubt of the fact that the railways of the United States have, in some respects, set a noble example to the rest of the world. They have introduced every possible source of economy into their system of transport, until they are now carrying the enormous freight traffic of the country at less than one-half the average rates that were current a few years ago. The result has been such a development of that traffic as the United States alone can show. The total ton-mileage of the freight carried on American railways in 1890 was not much short of equalling that of the whole of Europe, and was probably more than seven times that of the United Kingdom.* But the gross income from freight in that

* This must be largely a matter of estimate, inasmuch as the annual ton-mileage of British railways is not recorded. If, as some believe, the average lead is about thirty-five miles, the total ton-mileage of 1890 would be about 10,765 millions, which would be about one-seventh of the American ton-mileage in the same year.

year in the United States was only about 135 millions
sterling, as compared with 43¼ millions earned from the
same source by British railways, so that the American lines
did not earn much more than twice the gross revenue of
British lines, although they rendered probably about seven
times the amount of service.*   Obviously this means that
the American lines have been carrying traffic at very low
rates, so that whatever influence railway pools may have had
in other directions, they have not created a system of high
tariff charges, which is always injurious to the interests of
commerce.

A competent writer on traffic pools or allotments has
justly remarked that "not the least of the difficulties to be
met with in the administration of a great combination touch-
ing the material interests of the people at a thousand points,
is the fact that with the enlargement of its powers, it
becomes more and more amenable to public opinion, and
that when it assumes the form of a monopoly with respect
to any matter affecting the people generally, it becomes
subject to a degree of public accountability, almost, if not
quite, as decided as that which attaches to the administration of governmental affairs." †

Another serious difficulty that has almost uniformly
shortened the lives of combinations of this sort is that they
can only be founded upon the known circumstances existing
at the time.   But these circumstances are usually subject
to ultimate, and often to very rapid, change, and as these
changes cannot be foreseen or provided for, a revision of

---

* Being subject to the qualification stated above, this figure must not
be taken as absolute.

† Report on the Internal Commerce of the United States for 1879,
p. 182.

the terms of an agreement for pooling business is frequently called for. This revision is, of course, designed either to admit fresh parties to the pool, or to give some of the existing parties a larger share of business at the expense of others. This element of instability involves frequent re-construction of every pooling scheme, and a consequent liability to disruption.

The arguments against pooling have been well stated by Mr James F. Hudson, a well-known American writer on railway matters, who remarks that "the vital economic question of the day is whether great masses of capital shall be permitted the advantage of emancipating themselves from competition while subjecting the great body of those from whom they buy or sell to the most direct and powerful action of that force. The specious claim that the era of combination promises relief for the masses from the pressure of competition is wholly imaginative. If every department of trade and industry could be so equally subjected to the operation of trusts and pools that everybody —farmers, labourers, mechanics, merchants, and manufacturers—got just twice as much in wages and profits, the sum total of that change would be the reduction of the purchasing power of the dollar to the precious value of fifty cents. Every man's labour and enterprise would be exchanged for just as much of every other man's labour and enterprise as before. No such Utopian futility is contemplated in the prevalent efforts for the suspension of competition. The purpose of combination is to secure the suspension of competition in favour of the few, and to enable them to give less of the results of their labour and enterprise in exchange for the results of the labour and enterprise of the many.

" This involves the very foundation of democratic society

—equal rights and equal chances to secure the rewards of effort. It means privilege for those who are enabled to secure the abolition of competition in their own favour, while the mass of producers and consumers must sell to them or buy of them because under the pressure of that force. It contains that peril to free government pointed out by Daniel Webster fifty years ago in these words : ' The freest government, if it could exist, would not long be acceptable, if the tendency of the laws were to create a rapid accumulation of property in few hands and to render the great mass of the population dependent and penniless.'

"This principle is most vitally at stake in the proposition to permit and legalise railroad pools, although its presence may be somewhat obscured, more by the complicated nature of the machinery through which it acts than from any indirectness of its action. The idea of a 'trust' is abjured by the railway interest, but while the methods of organisation in trusts and pools are different, the distinctive and damnatory purpose of each is the same—that of smothering competition and arbitrarily securing a greater share of the rewards of production and distribution than would be permitted under the free action of that force. If the legislative power permits and upholds the means by which the great railway corporations propose to suspend competition and enhance the charges that enter into the cost of every staple, there is no public evil that can be inflicted by the trust that cannot be imposed on the public by legalised pools. The trust only came into existence because the pools, unrecognised by law, were futile. Make the pooling contract a legal one, and its public position will be exactly that of the trust, with its dangers and possibilities of extortion increased by the fact that it has a legal status, and that a combination of traffic is much more readily attainable than a combination of control or ownership.

"Prominent among the features of the effort to restore pooling is the sweeping and fearful indictment of the honesty and intelligence of railway management, and the remarkable allegations of utterly vicious corporate organisation, made by the railway interest itself. The most violent denunciations of the most radical anti-monopolists never formulated a more terrible arraignment than the declarations recently made that the rate-making power of the corporations is in irresponsible, reckless, and destructive hands. No attack upon the corporate system was ever a more sweeping indictment than the pooling assertion that if any railway is left to manage its own business, just as every great mercantile or manufacturing business must, the whole interest must fall into ruin.   No attack on the honesty and good faith of railroad management can be more bitter than the editorial declaration of a leading journal which advocates the pools, that 'the entire business is honeycombed with dishonesty and corruption, and every railroad president in the country more or less consciously connives at it.'   Even if these things were true they would offer no good reason for a remedy which would only emancipate those who are responsible for the evils from the natural and necessary penalty.   If railroads are organised on such vicious and irresponsible principles that they are conducted without regard to business principles, they should suffer the punishment." *

Whatever may with reason be urged against railway pooling arrangements from the point of view of the general public, they cannot be regarded as an unmixed evil.   When

* " *Bradstreet's* " December 15th, 1888.

they were first introduced into the railway economy of the
United States they were regarded with much disapproval.
Since then, however, it has been found that where such
pools are operated entirely by the companies themselves,
they have been the means of getting rid of discriminations
that were formerly very general, and which were calculated
seriously to prejudice, not only individual freighters, but,
by assisting to create monopolies, the general commercial
interests of the public.

There are, however, cases in which this salutary influence
not only does not come into play, but in which all the evils
of discrimination are likely to be seriously aggravated.
This is a general result of the method of pooling effected
through the agency of so-called "eveners"—usually large
freighters who keep the division of traffic agreed upon as
between the several lines even with, or equal to, the several
shares agreed upon. The eveners are generally allowed
certain compensation or return upon their own shipments,
which gives them a marked advantage over other shippers.
It was the position occupied as an "evener" by the Standard
Oil Company, in the coal-oil pool entered into by the trunk
lines between the oil regions and the seaboard, that gave
it its dominating superiority at an early stage in its history.

CHAPTER XV.

AMERICAN COAL POOLS.

In a previous chapter (p. 50), it has been shown that in the North of England, an arrangement known as "the vend" was in existence for many years during the earlier part of the century, for the purpose of controlling prices and production in the coal trade. It is perhaps a little singular that the methods of that organisation have not been copied elsewhere to a greater extent than appears to have been done. Generally speaking, with this notable exception, the coal trade has been remarkably free from the operation of any influences that would be likely to create artificial scarcity, and thereby enhance the range of prices, except such as have been created by the miners themselves in restricting their output. The trade has enjoyed—or perhaps, to put the matter more accurately, has suffered from, a fulness and completeness of competition that has been of the greatest possible benefit to the consumer, in placing at the disposal of national industry the cheapest and the best fuel supplies in Europe.

In the United States, however, several attempts have been made to interfere with the natural course of the coal industry—not in the trade as a whole, but in the anthracite region of Pennsylvania.

There is no single industry in the United States, equally concentrated, that has furnished such a large traffic to the railways of that country as the anthracite coal of Pennsylvania. The output of this description of coal in 1870 was 15½ million tons, and in 1890 it had risen to 42 million tons, being in the former year 45 per cent., and in the latter year 30 per cent., of the total production of coal in the country. Although the anthracite coal industry is practically limited to the comparatively small State of Pennsylvania, there are three divisions or sections of that State in which the industry is carried on, known severally as the Southern, the Northern, and the Middle coal-fields. The products of these several fields were, and are, marketed by different railways, which have engaged in a fierce competition for the transport of this valuable source of traffic over a number of years.

In 1872, in order to secure protection from the ruinous effects of this competition, the several railways engaged in it entered into an agreement to pool the traffic—that is, that each line should carry a certain definite proportion of the whole of the anthracite coal carried to what were known as competitive points, the exclusive control and management of its local trade being, however, retained by each. The pool continued in existence until the autumn of 1876. While it lasted, it almost necessarily excited a great deal of antagonism. The opponents of the pool maintained that the companies concerned had, in their competitive struggles, extended their plant much beyond the actual requirements of the trade, and declared that all such capital should share the common fate of depreciation in value which had fallen upon other property and other business enterprise throughout the country, whereas the railway managers, and the parties to the pooling arrangement generally, asserted that, while the pool continued, the prices of coal were not exces-

sive, and were only sufficiently high to maintain the usual
dividends on their properties.

One distinguishing feature of the anthracite pool of
1872-76 was that the railway companies controlled the production as well as the distribution of about 75 per cent. of the
total anthracite coal output of the country.   This they were
enabled to do in virtue of having secured the ownership of
that proportion of the coal-fields, either prior to, or during,
the existence of the pool.   Much opposition was naturally
offered to this action on the part of the railroads.   The
action was, however, defended on the ground that in no
other way than by the acquisition of the coal properties
could the railways prevent the protracted and frequently-
recurring periods of unbridled competition, during which the
prices of coal and the rates for its transportation failed to
yield a sufficient return.

In August 1876 the first anthracite coal pool came to
an end.   The reasons for the breakdown were various.
The several companies were not quite satisfied with the
proportions of the product allotted to each.   The Philadelphia and Reading secured over 28½ per cent. of the total
traffic, the Lehigh Valley Company 19¾ per cent., and the
Central Railroad of New Jersey about 13 per cent.   Apart,
however, from the jealousy and disruptive force inherent in
an arrangement of this kind, however well contrived, there
was the outside pressure of public opinion to reckon with.

A second coal combination was established in the Pennsylvania anthracite field in 1878.   During the interval since the
breakdown of the previous combination, the rates for the
transport of coal had been brought so low by competition
that the companies engaged in the business of production
and transport were unable to meet expenses.   The basis

of the second pool or apportionment was an agreement as
to the entire production and transport of all the anthracite
coal consumed in the coal regions, or shipped to points on
the lines of the several railroads.   A board of control was
appointed to see that the allotment made to each company
was duly carried out, and monthly adjustments under the
agreed division of business were made on the report of an
auditor as to the accounts of production and distribution.

The second anthracite pool was, however, only short-
lived.   It came to an end in December of 1878, mainly in
consequence of the refusal of one of the companies to
accept the terms offered and agreed upon by the other
companies.   This influence was aided in its operation by
the fact that, about the end of 1878, business began to im-
prove, and when that takes place, and when prices, under
the ordinary conditions of freedom of action and of contract, are fairly remunerative, there is generally a disinclination
on the part of capable business concerns to be fettered, as
they must be, by the conditions under which a combination
is established.

Several special circumstances distinguish the anthracite
coal combinations of Pennsylvania from any other concerns
of the like character that have ever been attempted.   In
the first place, it is important to remember that the owners
of the principal anthracite coal-fields were also the owners
of some of the principal lines of railway that ran through
them.   The object of the combination was twofold—to get
higher and more uniform prices for coal, as well as to have
a fuller command of rates of freight.   The organisation was
so constituted as to limit the quantity of coal produced,
and thereby to limit the amount of labour provided.   This
was an aspect of the case that provoked a great deal of

hostility on the part of private organisations and of State Legislatures alike. The most determined efforts were made again to break down the combination, but here also, as in the case of the great northern coal trade combination, the seeds of dissolution were sown from within, and not from without. The anthracite coal mining companies agreed that each should contribute a given proportion of the total quantity to be mined during the year, which total, of course, had previously been fixed. This arrangement was in force in 1873, 1874, and 1875, although there was a rebellion on the part of one important company, which refused to accept the allotment made to it. This, and the arrangements made by one or two other companies to sell a large quarttity of coal at auction, caused the combination to fall to pieces in August 1876. In 1878 another allotment combination was arranged, which, however, was dissolved in the following year, on its being found that one firm or company had been "cutting" rates, and another wanted a larger allotment. The dissolution of the anthracite combination was followed by a very remarkable fall in prices. The average price quoted for anthracite coals in 1879 was only two dollars thirty-three cents per ton. Four years previously it had been over five dollars per ton. In 1880 the combination was revived, and the average price rose to two dollars sixty-one cents per ton. For the four succeeding years, a combination of the companies producing and carrying anthracite coal was maintained, with a view to restricting quantity from time to time as might be required and thus to keep up prices. In 1884 a return was made to the allotment plan, under which each company was required to provide only a pre-arranged quota towards a definitely determined quantity. That quantity for the year 1885 was fixed at thirty millions of tons, but one of the principal companies objecting to its allotment, the combination was not successfully established.

There is no doubt that thirty millions of tons is a large quantity to pool, and it might be supposed that if thirty millions could be manipulated satisfactorily, so also could double or treble that quantity. But the circumstances of the anthracite coal trade are peculiar. Only eight large companies are engaged in it, and two of these companies had an allotment of 38·8 per cent., or more than one-third of the whole, while one company was only allotted 1½ per cent. This allotment is usually more or less arbitrary, and it is not a matter for surprise that companies which receive small allotments are liable to make a fuss. The anthracite coal trade is exceptional in another respect. The business is greatly centralised, being limited to a region covering about 1700 square miles, with a homogeneity and identity of interest that would probably not be found in any other locality. Indeed, it would be difficult, in the whole range of industry, to find a commodity so capable of lending itself to the manipulation of a pool as the anthracite coal of Pennsylvania. No safe inference can be drawn, therefore, from the history of this industry, unless it were that, even under the most favourable circumstances, such a combination was difficult.

In the early months of 1892, another combination, to which the Reading and Lehigh Valley Companies, and others engaged in the anthracite coal trade, were parties, was established for the purpose of obtaining a control over the production and prices of anthracite coal. The combination was, however, followed by legal proceedings intended to bring it to an end, the Court of Common Pleas for the State of Pennsylvania being asked by the Attorney-General for that State to find that the arrangements or leases made "were in contravention of the constitutional provisions in regard to parallel and competing lines of railroad, and to enjoin the parties thereto to refrain from carrying them out." A Committee of the New York Senate was at the same time appointed to inquire into the "deal," and in the course of the evidence laid before this Committee it was stated that the real object of the movement was "not to raise the price of coal, but to equalise it"—in consequence, it was said, of the fact, that in some localities coal was selling at too low, and in others at too high a price. Improved revenues were, however, expected from the introduction of economies and improvements in both production and distribution, and especially by "the avoidance of bidding against each other by the producers who were parties to the combination," without necessarily increasing the prices charged to consumers.

This combination was formed between the Reading, Jersey Central, and Lehigh Valley Railroads, with the promised co-operation of the Delaware Lackawanna, and Western and Delaware and Hudson Railroads. The combination came into practical effect in April 1892, and from that date until September coal prices advanced, in one case by as much as a dollar a ton. The avowed object of the Reading Company, which was the pioneer of the movement, was to secure a larger tonnage of coal at better prices. In the first year of the operation of the combination, the coal carried by the various anthracite railroads increased by nearly a million and a half tons, but the Reading group of lines carried fully one and one-eighth million tons less, so that the Reading Company did

not gain by the transaction. The other Companies, on
the contrary, carried about 2,750,000 tons more than they
had done in the year 1891. While the combination was
in existence, the shares of the combining Companies did
not increase in value, as might have been expected, but, on
the contrary, they all materially declined. The Reading
and the Lehigh Valley Railways were, in February 1893,
the only parties left of those who subscribed to the agreement a year before, the other lines having withdrawn.

CHAPTER XVI.

FUTURES AND CORNERS.

CLOSELY allied to the subjects we have been considering is the movement that has within recent years gained largely in volume and strength for the attainment of wealth by gambling in futures, by "cornering" the market, and by selling fictitious products—*i.e.*, products that are neither in the possession, nor at the disposal of, the seller.

It has been estimated by competent authorities that the stocks of all the principal commodities dealt with on the markets of the world, but notably wheat, cotton and iron, are liable to be constantly and seriously affected in price by transactions of the character indicated.

The main object aimed at by those who engage in operations of this sort is to obtain control of as much of the product which it is proposed to handle as is available, so that consumers, who must have supplies in order that they may keep their works or factories employed, or who must purchase for immediate requirements in other directions, may be required to pay a higher price than the normal average rate, the difference, of course, going into the pockets of the speculator. The operation of making a corner is usually, however, very risky for the operator. He must calculate the chances of his success with the utmost nicety, or he may easily find that he has been cornered himself.

L

It was announced in 1888 that a wealthy syndicate, having its head-quarters in Galveston, Texas, had made a more or less successful attempt to corner the two great American staples—wheat and cotton. As regards the former, the syndicate had bought an enormous quantity of wheat, said to be a million and a half bushels, at a price which netted about three cents a bushel all round, while they had nearly two million bushels more in the Chicago elevators, and held further contracts for about half a million bushels more. Although this syndicate bought wheat on a large scale at eighty-six cents a bushel in May, they made up their minds that they could realise one dollar twenty cents, or, say, 1s. 5d. per bushel, before they had held long. This syndicate made future contracts for 100,000 bales of cotton at Liverpool, New York, and New Orleans, and "closed out" some 20,000 bales in April 1888, at a net profit of four dollars a bale. This same syndicate was said to represent some ten million dollars of capital, and to embrace some of the largest capitalists in the United States. This, of course, gave it the command of large resources, and reduced the risk that is always run by those who attempt operations of this sort, that they may find themselves loaded with a supply of the commodity largely in excess of what they can dispose of, and consequently may be compelled to sell at a great sacrifice. Such a course has again and again been forced upon operators in both cotton and iron, and commercial disaster has been the nevitable result.

In September 1889, one of the most daring, and, on the whole, successful attempts that have ever been made to corner the cotton market was made by a Liverpool operator. So much anxiety did this attempt induce, that there was a general talk of closing the cotton mills in Lancashire, with a view to tide over the period of high prices created by the corner, until the new crop came to hand. This course of action was discussed on the hypothesis that the prices of manufactured cotton goods would fall rather than rise, and that the margin between the artificially high price of raw cotton, and the realised prices of cotton manufactures, would not be sufficient to enable manufacturers to live. But the speculator who had arranged for a corner, unlike the majority of the spinners, had made up his mind that the cotton crop of the year 1889 would be short, and on this theory he had made large purchases throughout the year. The event proved that he had judged the situation accurately. The prices of cotton goods improved as the year went on, and the operator who had so successfully diagnosed the outlook of the trade made large profits, to which he was not entirely without claim. Here, again, of course, the operator incurred large risks, at variance with that spirit of prudence and foresight which should control commercial operations. Had he been less accurate in his forecast, he would have been certain to come to grief.

In 1890, another attempt was made to carry out a cotton corner—this time, again, by the speculator who made the attempt in 1889. The gentleman in question is said to have agreed to purchase for spot and future delivery from 130,000 to 150,000 bales of American cotton. Spinners had, however, apparently in anticipation of some such movement, bought heavily in advance, and the price of raw cotton having fallen about three-farthings a pound in September, the would - be corner - maker found himself landed in a loss of £200,000 and bankruptcy. Gambling in this case met with the same fate that is almost sure eventually to overtake the gambler on the turf. The moth may dance about the flames for a while without hurt, but his wings are sure to get singed at last.

Only so recently as 1892 an attempt was made on a large scale to corner cotton in the United States, which was said to have large ramifications, and to have more or less of an international character. The Farmers' Alliance, it appears, had an *imperium in imperio* which was known as the Cotton Committee. This Committee was appointed by the Farmers' Alliance in the Southern States to formulate a plan that would enable cotton producers to hold their cotton for better prices. The members of the Committee, in pursuance of this end, proceeded to New York, and, it is said, held conferences with English capitalists with a view to establishing a gigantic corner in cotton. The *modus operandi* of the Committee may readily be understood from the following statement that appeared at the time in the *Journal of Finance* :—

" ' The National Alliance has achieved a great work. The Cotton Committee of the national body has completed arrangements with European capitalists to advance $32 per bale on 2,000,000 bales of American cotton, to be stored in the warehouses of the South for a period of one year, allowing the farmer to dispose of the cotton any time during the year should the price advance to his satisfaction.

" ' The European syndicate, which advances this money on the cotton, will charge 4 per cent. per annum interest, and will be fully secured by the cotton on which the advance is made. This arrangement means that the farmers will have the use of $64,000,000 and at the same time keep 2,000,000 bales of cotton out of the market. This money comes at the very lowest rate of interest that could be asked, and the arrangements cannot fail to produce a marked advance in the price of cotton, as it virtually withdraws at once over one-fourth of the crop of the country.

"'A year ago the Cotton Committee tried to make this arrangement with New York capitalists, and negotiations were almost completed to secure a like advance on 1,000,000 bales, but some little hitch occurred which upset the negotiations. This year the Committee sought Europe for capital, and everything is at last arranged.'

"Cotton merchants in this city, and bankers who have loans in the South, do not believe that the planters will ever carry their plan to consummation. They say that if a glimmer of common-sense does not reach them, then some other means may be found to prevent any such an extraordinary course. The reaction, they declare, once such a corner was broken, would cause widespread disaster. They doubt even that a corner could be made."

Innumerable cases of the same sort have happened on the Glasgow iron market. Speculation in pig iron warrants is notoriously one of the most common, and is regarded by not a few as one of the most hurtful and disturbing features of that important trade. The general effect of this form of speculation is that the speculator undertakes to sell what he is not possessed of, so that the operation has been described in law as a "wagering contract."

The movements of the Cotton Committee of the Farmers' Alliance was ostensibly designed to checkmate the operations of speculators and gamblers in "futures." In the State of Alabama the local delegation of the Alliance held a meeting in September 1892, and unanimously resolved to put their cotton on the market at the prices then current, at the same time calling upon the growers of cotton generally to follow the same course, and resist what was called the "unjust pressure" of buyers and others who looked to buying the crop at less than the usual price. The crop was declared by the farmers to be a short one, and they believed that if they could tide over a certain period without incurring obligations to their local bankers, which would compel them to sell at the low prices of the moment, they would ultimately secure a much better return. They therefore called upon the bankers and merchants in the Southern States to aid them in this endeavour, and thereby to "keep tillers of the soil from being robbed of their just reward, which would bring bankruptcy and ruin in the cotton belt." The attempt to make a corner in this way, however laudable from the point of view of the Farmers' Alliance, was only partially successful. The crop, being a short one, prices rose as a natural movement, and the returns to the cotton-growers were extremely satisfactory, but this was not at all due to an artificial operation.

" Wagering contracts," within which are included all contracts for differences, were not illegal at common law, and were first dealt with by statute of 8 and 9 Victoria, c. 109. By section 18 of this Act it is provided as follows : " That all contracts or agreements, whether by parol or in writing, by way of gaming or wagering, shall be null and void ; and that no suit shall be brought or maintained in any court of law or equity for recovering any sum of money or valuable thing alleged to be won upon any wager "—the rest being immaterial to the case under consideration.

On this section, Mr Benjamin, Q.C., in his work on "Sales," says : " Such a contract "—*i.e.*, for the sale of goods to be delivered at a future day—" is only valid where the parties really intend and agree that the goods are to be delivered by the seller, and the price to be paid by the buyer. If under guise of such a contract the real intent be merely to speculate in the rise or fall of prices, and the goods are not to be delivered, but one party is to pay to the other the difference between the contract price and the market price of the goods at the date fixed for the execution of the contract, then the whole transaction constitutes nothing more than a wager, and is null and void under the statute."

There are two cases which put a liberal construction upon this section ; but against these more authoritative decisions exist which go to show that the dictum of Mr Benjamin is, though strictly correct, of little value in practice.

In the cases of Grizewood v. Blane and Cooper v. Neil, it was left to the jury to say what, under the circumstances, was "the intention of the parties as understood by both of them"—whether they contemplated a sale or a mere bet upon the price, and the jury coming to the conclusion that the contract was a mere wager, the contract was declared void under the statute.

The case of Thacker v. Hardy, decided by the Court of Appeal in 1878, may, however, be considered to throw considerable doubt upon the preceding cases. The action was one by a stockbroker to recover commission, and to obtain an indemnity from his principal in respect of speculations of the kind known as "time bargains" upon the Stock Exchange. The defence was that the transactions were "gaming and wagering" transactions, and so void within section 18 of 8 and 9 Vic., c. 109. The Court of Appeal (Bramwell, Brett, and Cotton, L.J.J.) affirming, Lindlay, J. (now L.J.), held that the plaintiff was entitled to recover, for "the employment of the plaintiff by the defendant was not against public policy, and was not illegal at common law, and, further, was not in the nature of a gaming and wagering contract against the provisions of 8 and 9 Vic., c. 109, section 18."

Broadly stated, this judgment declares :

1. That the contract between the principal employing a broker and the broker is good.

2. That the contract made by the broker for his principal to buy or to sell is good.

Lindlay, J., in the course of his judgment, said that " the case of a real time bargain, such as would be touched by the statute, was, he suspected, very rare.   What were generally called ' time bargains ' were, in fact, the result of two distinct and perfectly legal bargains, viz., first, a bargain to buy or sell ; and, secondly, a subsequent bargain that the first shall not be carried out ; and it was only when the first bargain was entered into with the understanding that it was not to be carried out, that a time bargain in the sense of an unenforcable bargain was entered into."

It will be observed that the decision in Thacker *v.* Hardy leaves untouched the question whether a "time bargain," of the kind ordinarily entered into, is good as between principal and principal ; and it should be remembered that in betting cases very important differences have been drawn between the case of principals betting and bets through agents, it being held in the latter case that where the agent has paid a bet he can recover it against his principal, although the actual bet is not legal.   But it may well be questioned whether an ordinary time bargain between principals, the purchaser having the option of taking up the stock, would not be declared good, especially as we have the view of Lindley, J., that a time bargain such as would be covered by the statute is "a very rare occurrence"; and the question of the intent of the parties—whether the sale was *bona fide* or gambling—would in any case be referred to the jury as a question of fact; and it is found with a jury of commercial men very difficult to get them to say that an ordinary time bargain is a wager.

Mr F. T. Piggott, the author of some well-known text-books, is of opinion that had the Stock Exchange rules, making the broker a principal, been present to the minds of the Court, they would have held that the contract even of the broker was void; but this is assuming that Grizewood *v.* Blane is good law, and so far from approving this decision, as Mr Piggott says the Court of Appeal did, they avoid deciding the question as between principal and principal.

When a contract is to be regarded as a wagering transaction, and not as a valid contract for the sale and delivery of property is a question which is coming before the courts frequently under modern business conditions. One of the latest decisions bearing upon the question has recently been rendered by the Supreme Court of Nebraska in a suit brought by a Chicago broker against a Nebraska speculator on a note given to cover margins. The Court held that where there was no intention on the part of an alleged buyer to purchase or to receive grain, and no intention on the part of an alleged seller to deliver the same, no recovery could be had upon the contract. It further held that though the outward forms of law may have been complied with in such cases, yet where the defence is that the contract is a wagering one, it is the duty of the courts to go behind the contract and to examine the facts to ascertain its true character. The view of the law taken by the Nebraska court is in line with the current of the best considered authorities.   It does not declare transactions in "futures" or "options" as such to be wagering transactions, but does class in that category transactions in which there is no intention on the part of either party to make a *bona fide* purchase or sale.

Mr Justice Fenner, of the Supreme Court of the State of Louisiana, has thus stated the difficulties in the way of dealing with speculation in futures and cornering the market :—

"(1) Sales of property for future delivery, with the *bona fide* intention and obligation to make actual delivery, are lawful contracts, but if, under the form of such a contract, the real intent be merely to speculate upon the rise and fall of prices, and the goods are not to be delivered, but the contract to be suited on the basis of difference of price, the transaction is a wager, and is non-actionable.

"(2) In order to affect the contract, the alleged illegal intent must have been mutual, and such intent by one party, not concurred in by the other, will not avail.

"(3) The law presumes lawful purpose until the contrary is proved, and when one party charges illegal intent, the burden of proof is imposed upon him.

"(4) The validity of the contract depends upon the state of things existing at its date, and is not affected by subsequent agreements under which the parties voluntarily assent to a settlement on the basis of differences.

"(5) The mere fact that at the date of his contract the vendor had not the goods, and had made no arrangement for receiving them, does not suffice to impair the contract."

The business in "futures" in the different commercial centres in Europe and America has hitherto been confined to a few important articles, as grain, cotton, sugar, coffee, and spirits, in which a large number are interested both as producers and consumers, and in which the production, being dependent upon the weather, fluctuates considerably from year to year.

The advantages which " futures " afford to commerce, and to the consumers and producers, as such, briefly stated, are as follows :—

The rise and fall in prices is not so considerable, since any unforeseen circumstance, even the smallest, may affect them. When there appears to be every prospect of a good harvest the producer can sell for later delivery at a favourable price, whereas, if he were to wait until his products were in a fit condition to be delivered, he would have to accept a lower price. On the other hand, when the consumer sees that, owing to the increased demand, he will have to pay a higher price later on, he can cover his future requirements at a time when prices are still low, whereas, if he deferred buying and the stocks became reduced, he would have to pay much more.

With the introduction of the telegraph, all the countries where an article is produced and consumed have been brought into instant communication with each other. Not the least incident or the slightest fluctuation occurs in one country but it immediately becomes known in all the rest. Hence it results that the commercial world in the present day is in a far better position to form a correct judgment than was the case when news could only travel by post, for the condition of things might have totally changed in the interval between the despatch and the receipt of a letter.

Owing to the greatly improved and accelerated means of communication, it has become possible to transport much quicker than formerly large quantities of goods from one country, where a superfluity of an article prevails, to another country where it is much needed. Two results are thereby produced. By the withdrawal of goods from the country where they are superabundant, a great depreciation is avoided, while by transferring them to another country where there is a scarcity, an excessive rise of prices in the latter is prevented. As, however, the goods cannot be so quickly removed from place to place as the order for their sale or purchase can be transmitted by telegraph, it follows that there must be buying and selling for future delivery. This answers the purpose of the consumer, who may be at the present moment sufficiently provided with the article, but will require more of it subsequently for his future needs.

At the session of Congress held in February 1889, bills to punish dealing in futures in agricultural products, and to prohibit fictitious and gambling transactions on the prices of articles produced by American farm industry, were introduced in the House of Representatives. These bills were for some time under consideration by the Committee on Agriculture, to which they were referred. That Committee has reported the bills adversely. It has arrived at the conclusion, among others, that Congress has no jurisdiction over the subject, and that the limitations imposed by the Constitution make it improper for Congress to pass the measures proposed, which, the Committee holds, are matters for State legislation exclusively.

The Glasgow warrant market, as everybody knows, is one that readily lends itself to the making of rigs and corners from its very character, but it is nevertheless a fact that very few such operations have been carried out successfully, so that prices are rarely controlled by the artificial agencies alluded to. There is, no doubt, a large amount of speculation carried on in warrants, and all sorts and conditions of men have tried a "flyer" in warrants with the view of "making a bit of money," with results that are as frequently disastrous as successful. But such a thing as a really dominant rig is almost unknown. And, on the whole, the business done on the Glasgow warrant market is not a matter for deprecation so long as the game is confined to those who understand the value of the counters. On the contrary, it has been remarked, in a leading journal, that "the transactions on this market range from five to ten millions of tons a year, and are settled with an amount of promptitude, and an absence of loss from default, that reflects the highest credit on the dealers." It has been suggested in Glasgow that protection could be secured against the influence of a rig by appointing somebody who should have power to suspend the settlement of transactions whenever a rig is attempted, holding the seller liable for any loss incurred by the buyer from being unable to provide iron actually required.

Many attempts have been made to corner the pig-iron warrant market in Glasgow, but only very few have succeeded. One of the most notable of these was made in the year 1866, when a body of speculators for the rise combined to resist the "bears," and drove up the price of pig-iron from 65s. to 80s. At the higher price they tried to get rid of their stock, but failed ignominiously. The consequence was that very serious losses were incurred in disposing of the produce that had been cornered, and with scarcely a single exception the parties to the attempt became ruined. One of the journals of the time, in commenting on the transaction, remarked fairly enough that "no sympathy was wasted on them (the speculators), because it was held that a combination or operation, with the view of forcing a seller to buy back what the purchasers have rendered it impossible that he can deliver, is a fraudulent transaction, illegal and immoral in its very nature."

In 1873, some wealthy speculators in Dundee and Glasgow attempted to repeat the experiment of 1866, in the way of trying to prop up a falling market. The condition of trade at that time was both curious and critical. Pig-iron had been forced up to as much as 160s. per ton, due in part to the serious increase in the price of coal and in the cost of labour, but also to some extent as the result of speculative activity. In Scotland, a number of works engaged in the production of malleable or wrought iron had to close their gates in consequence of their inability to produce at the then current price of pig. As often happens, the price of finished iron had failed to keep abreast of that of the raw material used in its manufacture, and when this became a marked characteristic of the situation the demand for pig-iron, and its price, alike showed a fall. It was then that an attempt was made to create a "corner" to keep up the price of iron, by acquiring the command of the stocks in the Glasgow warrant stores, but no better result attended the operation than had attended similar operations before. The price of pig-iron continued to fall, and it has never attained the same high level since. The usual impotence of any attempt to force back the current of a falling market was attended by the usual disastrous results to the experimenters.

Happily, for the protection of the general public, the penalties that are liable to attend unsuccessful attempts at cornering a market are so serious and crushing as to quench the ardour of all but the most reckless speculators on behalf of such an enterprise.

CHAPTER XVII.

INTERNATIONAL REGULATION OF PRICES.

HITHERTO we have spoken only of the regulation of prices and of production as carried out in one country only, and as affecting only the special circumstances of that country. In all such cases, we have seen that the tendency of a limitation of output, and of a consequently artificial advance of price, is to restrict consumption, to create means of supply in foreign countries, and to invite and assist the competition of foreign sources of supply in neutral markets, and probably in our own.

It is, however, possible to overcome the two latter difficulties to a large extent, if not entirely, by the adoption of an international agreement to sell the same product in all outside markets at the same prices, and so to get rid, for the time being, of the existence of competition, in so far as the regulated product is concerned.

Obviously, this is a very much wider and more comprehensive plan of operation, and one that calls for the exercise of more tact, judgment, and discretion, as well as of a higher organising faculty. If the rocks upon which the attempt to regulate one industry, affecting only one country, are likely to split appear to be both many and formidable, how much more formidable must be the obstacles that lie in the path of a movement designed to harmonise and coordinate the interests of different countries, which are in their essence, their aims, and their traditions so essentially antagonistic?

And yet, when one comes to reflect apon the matter, there are comparatively few industries that may not, under proper conditions and treatment, be dealt with in this way. The basis of such an arrangement would naturally be of a two-fold character : the first, that each country subscribing to the agreement should have undisputed possession of its home market ; the next, that the price to be quoted by the competing countries to outside or neutral markets should be always, and under all circumstances, the same.

As regards the first of these conditions, there should be little or no difficulty in giving it effect. All countries that are in a position to be parties to such an arrangement have already taken measures to protect more or less completely their own home markets. Our own country is, no doubt, *nominally* an exception to this rule. But there are more forms of protection than one, and a national industry may be effectually protected without raising around it the doubtfully adequate bulwarks of high tariffs. England has no artificial protection for her industries, like most other manufacturing nations ; but she has what may be, and to a large extent undoubtedly is, a more efficient shield against foreign competition in the form of efficient labour, cheap materials, great technical skill, and a consequently low cost of production. Most other countries, whether with or without these advantages, take care to protect themselves by levying duties on imported commodities.

The home market, therefore, is hardly in question. But the home market might be, and probably would be, in question, if prices were raised artificially to such an extent as to reduce the differences of price that now keep our competitors at bay. In other words, it is generally dangerous to advance the prices of commodities in any one country without arranging that the same commodities, if of a highly competitive character, shall be advanced equally in other countries. In all such cases, it is well to "agree quickly with thine adversary."

As regards neutral markets, supposing that the home market were adequately protected, it might be easily possible to secure a high price at home, and to quote a low price abroad. This, in point of fact, is being done at the present time in Germany, Austria, and some other countries. The iron manufacturers of Germany regularly adopt two sets of prices. The tariff, by protecting them from outside competition, enables them to quote a high range of prices —which are often regulated by combination—to home consumers, while they dispose of a large surplus, at a lower range of prices, in neutral markets where they have to face the competition of other countries. It is under such circumstances that England has to compete with Germany in many outside markets.

To follow out the case already cited, it is clear that Germany cannot hope to obtain in neutral markets a higher price than England ; so that, if she is to secure business at all, she must quote a lower price than the lowest price tendered by England for the same description of goods. Hence the price that secures the business is generally one that is far from being adequately remunerative to the producer, and not infrequently one that involves a considerable loss in the manufacture.*   In short, it is the constant tend-

* To a country that is able to secure, like Germany, higher prices at home, the one price will balance the other to a large extent ; but a

M

ency of unrestricted competition to depress prices to an irreducible minimum, which is generally excellent for the consumer, but often far from satisfactory to the producer.

When, therefore, competitive countries can agree upon an uniform price for the same commodities in all non-competitive countries, they are likely to benefit equally by the arrangement, although the need of one country may not be quite so urgent as the need of another, so that the higher price may be to one a mere incident, and to the other a matter of life or death.

An international combination may, of course, be carried much further even than this. The proportions of the total product of a commodity to be furnished by each country may be fixed beforehand, involving, as a necessary detail, the fixing of the proportions towards the total of each country to be supplied by each individual manufacturer, and the proportions of the total annual requirements of each neutral or non-competitive market to be supplied by each competing country may be similarly fixed and determined.

Unless some such arrangement as the first-named were adopted, there would be likely to be a speedy glut of the commodity, and there would thereupon be likely to arise an irresistible temptation on the part of the weaker firms to accept lower prices than those which formed the basis of the arrangement. Not only so, but the financial incubus of a great surplus of output would be likely to so far depress any trade carried on under such conditions, that it would inevitably cause the combination to fall to pieces. In the case of the syndicate formed a few years ago for the purpose of controlling production and prices in the steel rail trade,

country like England has no such offset, and hence would appear to have more to gain from a regulated price.

the combination fixed precisely the quantity of rails that should be contributed by each individual firm towards the filling up of the orders known to be in the market, so that there was no likelihood of weakening the arrangement by the anxiety or necessity to dispose of an accumulation of stocks.*

In an international arrangement, however, if carried up to this point, there are two inherent elements of weakness that have never been overcome successfully for any great length of time. The first is due to the difficulty of fixing the quantities to be supplied to non-competitive markets by each country; the second to the difficulty of satisfying the individual firms concerned, in the matter of their allotments. It is natural, for example, that each country should believe in, and stand for, its inalienable right to have the whole of its own colonial business without the intrusion of foreign sources of supply. English manufacturers would be slow to admit the claim of Germans to secure a large slice of our trade with Canada, Australia, or the Cape, but if the competitive country has already secured a slice of such trade, the fact must be recognised and provided for in any ulterior arrangement that is designed to allocate the trade for the future. Such an allocation could only reasonably proceed upon the percentage of the trade of a neutral market already secured, and during the existence of such a combination, that proportion would be likely to remain stationary, no matter

* In the case of this organisation, the resources of production, both in England and on the Continent, were very much in excess of the actual demand for rails, but the quota of each firm having once been fixed, there was an honourable understanding that no more should be produced.

how much, in the natural order of events, the proportion should be increased or diminished. The alternative presented to this condition is that of possibly seeing a competitive country increase its hold upon the markets that are in dispute, at a cut-throat range of prices.

It is, perhaps, even more difficult to arrive at a satisfactory arrangement of the proportions which each individual firm should contribute to the grand total required to satisfy the demands of the world, in so far as they are either affected, or liable to be affected, by competition. In fixing such proportions two obvious considerations must have great, if not absolutely controlling weight, namely :—

1. The extent of the works and their known capacity of production, and

2. The extent to which that capacity has been utilised in executing orders already received.

The process known as the "higgling of the market" must, to a large extent, come into play in a matter of this sort, but at the best, the process of adjustment is a difficult one, and generally leads to the more or less pronounced failure of all attempts to combine manufacturers for regulative purposes, whether as a national or as an international organisation.

Of course, in these matters, the consumer is put in the second place, if he is regarded at all. It is only when the natural operation of the law of supply and demand tends to give the consumer advantages which the producer cannot afford, that the latter seeks for this form of protection, and when he does, he generally has the consuming interest arrayed against him—to such an extent, indeed, that orders are withheld as far as they possibly can be.

This, again, becomes a serious element of weakness, inasmuch as the anticipated benefits of organisation are countervailed by reduced demand, and, being spread over a smaller output, are not supposed to compensate for the loss of individual liberty which is involved in meeting the conditions on which such an organisation is alone possible.

Not many attempts have been made to establish international combinations of this kind on a large scale. In a general way, the area of operations, and the natural antagonism of the interests involved are such as to make such organisations difficult, but the steel rail trade was successfully syndicated by agreement between England, Belgium, and Germany for a year or two, under circumstances which at least demonstrated that the experiment need not necessarily prove a failure.

CHAPTER XVIII.

THE EVILS OF THE TRUST SYSTEM.

In the course of the preceding pages, so much has been said by way of showing the evils that have attended the establishment of the system of trusts, and the difficulties of carrying on such organisations with a view to the advantage either of their own members or of the general public, that it will hardly be expected that we should go very fully over the ground covered by these considerations.

Briefly stated, the principal objections brought against the trust system are that it tends to establish monopoly, to crush small manufacturers and producers, to place vast wealth in the hands and at the disposal of irresponsible individuals, to increase the prices of necessary commodities, to dislocate and disturb labour, and to generally unsettle the relations and prospects of commerce and industry.

That Trusts are not, in their essence and principles, institutions calculated to command popular confidence and approval is sufficiently established by the crusade that has been undertaken against them in the United States. Within the last four or five years, measures have been proposed for limiting their powers, or compelling their abandonment, in all the principal American States. Indeed, it has been asserted that of late years they have become a subject of much more public attention than the Tariff itself, and that the slow progress made by the

Republican party in getting them crushed out was one of the most potent influences in the movement that brought back the Democrats to place and power.   Not only so, but the general law against Trusts adopted by the Government of the United States in 1892, at the instance of Senator John Sherman, was, in many quarters, regarded as one of the most wise and desirable measures of the kind hitherto introduced into the American Legislature, and it seldom happens that the public indignation is aroused against any movement or system that has, on the face of it, obvious and overwhelming merits.   The Trust system has in short been an abstract Ishmaelite, against whom every man's hand has been raised.

The General Laws Committee of the State Senate of New York, in a Report made on the 6th of March 1888, has an emphatic condemnation of the system of Trusts. "However different the influences which give rise to these combinations may be, the main purpose and effect of all upon the public is the same, to wit—the aggregation of capital, the power of controlling the manufacture and output of various necessary commodities, the acquisition or destruction of competitive properties—all leading to the final and conclusive purposes of annihilating competition and enabling the combinations to fix the price at which they would purchase the raw material from the producer, and at which they would sell the refined product to the consumer.   In any event the public at each end of the industry is, and is intended to be, in a certain sense, at the mercy of the syndicate, combination, or trust."   The conditions under which, and the terms upon which, the various principal trusts are established, are then criticised with a view to proving that these animadversions are fully called for. Nor is this surprising when we consider the portentous extent of the evil complained of and the circumstances of its recent growth.

Professor Hadley remarks that "nearly every industry in the United States employing fixed capital on a large scale has its pool, whether they call it by that name or not. The Anthracite Coal Combination has been less successful than the Standard Oil Company, but its method of crushing small rivals by denying them transportation facilities has made it almost equally notorious. And now the system of combination has extended to other regions besides the anthracite. Again, every branch of hardware, from rails to carpet tacks, has its combination to keep up prices or restrict production. The cases are only too frequent where the combination pays certain mills for *not* running, more than they could earn by running. For lumber and for paper, for cattle and for milk, for cartridges and for matches —in each business there is an organised combination, fixing rates and often limiting production. The waterways themselves, which, we are so often assured, are to protect us from the monopoly of the railroads, have their rates fixed and their traffic pooled by combinations of greater or lesser influence—from the local barge association of some interior town to the great North Atlantic Conference. How much freight each of the leading steamships is to carry is not infrequently made the subject of agreement with the owners of rival vessels."

With the exception of the Standard Oil Trust, and perhaps one or two others that rose somewhat earlier, it may be fairly said, in the opinion of Professor Jenks,*

* On Trusts in the United States, in the *Economic Journal*, March 1892, p. 73.

"that not merely competition, but competition that was proving ruinous to many establishments, was the cause of the combinations.   It seemed the only way by which not extortionate, but fair, profits could be made.   This remark does not apply to a number of later organisations, formed of establishments which, although already making good profits, hoped and expected to obtain better—not so much in the saving of the cost of production, as by high charges to be paid by the consumer.   It is this latter fact, more perhaps than any other, that has caused the loud outcry against the system.   If those who took it up had been limited to the industries or establishments that suffered from the effects of over-production and unhealthy conditions of competition, the popular tumult would never have reached the height that it has done, but the system has been largely abused, and abused at the cost of the general public, both as a producer and as a consumer."

One of the principal and most popular objections brought against the trust system is that it tends to "stifle labour"—to unsettle wages and employment.

This argument has been answered by Mr John H. Flagler, by the assertion that, under the Trust system, such a thing as a strike is unknown, and no differences have arisen between employer and employed.*   He asserts also that it is the weakness of small manufacturers, who have to succumb to the law of the survival of the fittest, that leads to "disaster, suspension of manufacture, stoppage of employment, and general dissatisfaction."†

It is probable, moreover, that the apprehension of what

* This statement, made in 1888, may not be equally true at the present time.

† Address to the Commercial Club of Providence.

the trust system might ultimately lead to in the way of limiting the supply of commodities and artificially increasing their price, has had as much to do with their condemnation as the mischief they have actually done, whether that mischief be large or small in amount. Naturally enough, the public became timid lest the movement should spread beyond controllable bounds, not realising that the evils that were mostly feared were likely to cure themselves.

Professor Hadley,* referring to the growth of the Standard Oil Trust, remarks that "the public are alarmed at the growth of such a power in their midst—able, apparently, to dictate the price of a necessary of life, and subject to no restraint or control from outside. Statesmen, lawyers, and journalists held up their hands in holy horror; and exclaimed, Can such things be?"

* Railroad Transportation, p. 68.

INDEX.

A

ADVANTAGE of "futures," 170
Agricultural products, trusts in, 73
Alkali industry, trust in the, 118
Allhusen, C., remarks on chlorine by, 120
Allotment of proportions, 65
American coal pools, 153 ; anthracite pool of 1872-76, 155 ; pool of 1878, 156 ; special circumstances, 156 ; pool of 1892, 158
—— v. Scotch oil producers, 92
—— cotton corners, 164
Ammonia soda process, 119
Anthracite coal combination denounced, 40
Australian shipping trade, ring in the, 124 ; demands made by, 127 ; competition of Continental ports, 128 ; freight rings, 129 ; Mogul Shipping Company, 130

B

Badgering, definition of, 12
Bastiat's aphorisms as to buyers and sellers, 11 ; definition of competition, 28
Benjamin, Q. C., on wagering contracts, 166
Bleaching Powder Association, 120, 123
Buckle on European Governments, 8

Brewery trust in United States, 134
British Coal v. American, 67
Brokers and principals, 168

C

Cases of agreements to prevent competition quoted, 34
Causes of industrial depressions, 27
Chemical trust, 118
Coal trade of the north of England, syndicates in the, 50 ; low prices in, 54
—— producing districts compared, 63
—— pool, proposed in 1888 for United Kingdom, 61
—— trusts, German, 137 ; American, 153
Coke-makers' combination, 139
Combinations regarded as monopolies, 15
Competition, definition of by Bastiat, 28
Commodities, increase of cost of, 30
Competition, 28 ; stimulus of, 29
Comptoir d' Escompte, 115
Corners, 161
Copper trust, history of, 112 ; effect of on prices, 113 ; attitude of buyers, 114 ; failure of, 114 ; collapse of prices, 114 ; attitude

TURNBULL AND SPEARS, PRINTERS, EDINBURGH.

A LIST OF NEW BOOKS AND ANNOUNCEMENTS OF METHUEN AND COMPANY PUBLISHERS : LONDON 36 ESSEX STREET W.C.

CONTENTS

JANUARY 1895

MESSRS. METHUEN'S
ANNOUNCEMENTS

———◆———

Poetry

Rudyard Kipling. BALLADS. By RUDYARD KIPLING. *Crown 8vo. Buckram.* 6s.

The announcement of a new volume of poetry from Mr. Kipling will excite wide interest. The exceptional success of 'Barrack-Room Ballads,' with which this volume will be uniform, justifies the hope that the new book too will obtain a wide popularity.

W. E. Henley. ENGLISH LYRICS. Selected and Edited by W. E. HENLEY. *Crown 8vo. Buckram.* 6s.

    Also 30 copies on hand-made paper *Demy 8vo.* £1, 1s.

    Also 15 copies on Japanese paper. *Demy 8vo.* £2, 2s.

Few announcements will be more welcome to lovers of English verse than the one that Mr. Henley is bringing together into one book the finest lyrics in our language. Robust and original the book will certainly be, and it will be produced with the same care that made 'Lyra Heroica' delightful to the hand and eye.

"Q" THE GOLDEN POMP: A Procession of English Lyrics from Surrey to Shirley, arranged by A. T. QUILLER COUCH. *Crown 8vo. Buckram.* 6s.

    Also 30 copies on hand-made paper. *Demy 8vo.* £1, 1s.

    Also 15 copies on Japanese paper. *Demy 8vo.* £2, 2s.

Mr. Quiller Couch's taste and sympathy mark him out as a born anthologist, and out of the wealth of Elizabethan poetry he has made a book of great attraction.

H. C. Beeching. LYRA SACRA : An Anthology of Sacred Verse. Edited by H. C. BEECHING, M.A. *Crown 8vo. Buckram.* 6s.

This book will appeal to a wide public. Few languages are richer in serious verse than the English, and the Editor has had some difficulty in confining his material within his limits.

W. B. Yeats. A BOOK OF IRISH VERSE. Edited by W. B. YEATS. *Crown 8vo.* 3s. 6d.

An anthology of Irish poetry selected by an editor whose own verse has won a considerable reputation.

Fiction

MESSRS. METHUEN call attention to the fact that the following novels are issued for the first time in one volume instead of in the old two and three volume form.

Gilbert Parker. THE TRAIL OF THE SWORD. By GILBERT PARKER, Author of 'Pierre and his People,' etc. *Crown 8vo.* 6s.

A historical romance dealing with the stirring period in the history of Canada in which France and England were contending for its possession.

Anthony Hope. A MAN OF MARK. By ANTHONY HOPE, Author of 'The Prisoner of Zenda,' 'The God in the Car,' etc. *Crown 8vo.* 6s.

This is a re-issue of Anthony Hope's first novel. It has been out of print for some years, and in view of the great popularity of the author, it has been reprinted. It is a story of political adventure in South America, and is rather in the style of 'The Prisoner of Zenda.'

Mrs. Clifford. A FLASH OF SUMMER. By MRS. W. K. CLIFFORD, Author of 'Aunt Anne,' etc. *Crown 8vo.* 6s.

This is the first long story which Mrs. Clifford has written since the remarkably successful 'Aunt Anne.'

M. M. Dowie. GALLIA. By MENE MURIEL DOWIE. Author of 'A Girl in the Carpathians.' *Crown 8vo.* 6s.

This is a story of modern society by the author of 'A Girl in the Carpathians,' which was probably one of the most popular books of travel ever published.

Mrs. Oliphant. SIR ROBERT'S FORTUNE. By MRS. OLIPHANT. *Crown 8vo.* 6s.

Mrs. Pinsent. CHILDREN OF THIS WORLD. By ELLEN F. PINSENT, Author of 'Jenny's Case.' *Crown 8vo.* 6s.

A story of modern life and thought, being a study of two opposite types—the Christian and the Agnostic. Mrs. Pinsent's first book was very successful, and the leading critics spoke of it as a remarkable and powerful story, and as one which made them look forward with keen interest to the author's next book.

W. E. Norris. THE DESPOTIC LADY AND OTHERS. By W. E. NORRIS, Author of 'The Rogue,' etc. *Crown 8vo.* 6s.

E. F. Benson. LADY MASSINGTON'S RESURRECTION, AND OTHER STORIES. By E. F. BENSON, Author of 'Dodo.' *Crown 8vo.* 6s.

Julian Corbett. A BUSINESS IN GREAT WATERS. By
JULIAN CORBETT, Author of 'For God and Gold,' 'Cophetua
XIIIth.,' etc. *Crown 8vo. 6s.*

This is a historical romance of the time of the French Revolution by a writer whose
previous stories have been much praised for their 'romantic beauty and profound
interest and nervous strength of style.' Many critics noticed their 'wholesome
freshness' and 'vivid reproduction of the past.'

Gilbert Parker. AN ADVENTURER OF THE NORTH.
By GILBERT PARKER, Author of 'Pierre and his People,' 'The
Translation of a Savage,' etc. *Crown 8vo. 6s.*

This book consists of more tales of the Far North, and contains the last adventures
of 'Pretty Pierre.' Mr. Parker's first volume of Canadian stories was published
about two years ago, and was received with unanimous praise.

Philipps-Woolley. THE QUEENSBERRY CUP. A Tale of
Adventure. By CLIVE PHILIPPS WOOLLEY, Author of 'Snap,' Part
Author of 'Big Game Shooting.' Illustrated. *Crown 8vo. 6s.*

This is a story of amateur pugilism and chivalrous adventure, written by an author
whose books on sport are well known.

Miss Benson. SUBJECT TO VANITY. By MARGARET
BENSON. With numerous Illustrations. *Crown 8vo. 3s. 6d.*

A volume of humorous and sympathetic sketches of animal life and home pets.

NEW EDITIONS

Anthony Hope. THE GOD IN THE CAR. By ANTHONY
HOPE, Author of 'A Change of Air,' etc. *Sixth Edition. Crown
8vo. 6s.*

'This is, indeed, a very remarkable book, deserving of critical analysis impossible
within our limits ; brilliant, but not superficial ; well considered, but not elaborated ; constructed with the proverbial art that conceals, but yet allows itself to be
enjoyed by readers to whom fine literary method is a keen pleasure ; true without
cynicism, subtle without affectation, humorous without strain, witty without
offence, inevitably sad, with an unmorose simplicity.'—*World.*

'Immeasurably better than anything Mr. Hope has done before. A novel eminently
worth reading, full of brilliance, fire, and daring.'—*Manchester Guardian.*

'Ruston is drawn with extraordinary skill, and Maggie Dennison with many subtle
strokes. The minor characters are clear cut. In short the book is a brilliant one.
"The God in the Car" is one of the most remarkable works in a year that has
given us the handiwork of nearly all our best living novelists.'—*Standard.*

Baring Gould. KITTY ALONE. By S. BARING GOULD,
Author of 'Mehalah,' 'Cheap Jack Zita,' etc. *Second Edition.
Crown 8vo. 6s.*

'If any one wants—and in days when so much fiction is morbid and depressing it is
to the credit of human nature to believe that many persons must want—a book
brisk, clever, keen, healthy, humorous, and interesting, he can scarcely do better
than order "Kitty Alone."'—*National Observer.*

Norris. MATTHEW AUSTIN. By W. E. NORRIS, Author of 'Mdle. de Mersac,' etc. *Second Edition. Crown 8vo. 6s.*

'It would be a strangely unsympathetic and cynical person who could read the life-story of Matthew Austin, the singularly unselfish and gentle-natured country doctor, without affectionate sympathy . . . "Matthew Austin" may safely be pronounced one of the most intellectually satisfactory and morally bracing novels of the current year.'—*Daily Telegraph.*

Mrs. Watson. THIS MAN'S DOMINION. By the Author of 'A High Little World.' *Second Edition. Crown 8vo. 3s. 6d.*

'It is not a book to be read and forgotten on a railway journey, but it is rather a study of the perplexing problems of life, to which the reflecting mind will frequently return, even though the reader does not accept the solutions which the author suggests. In these days, when the output of merely amusing novels is so overpowering, this is no slight praise. There is an underlying depth in the story which reminds one, in a lesser degree, of the profundity of George Eliot, and "This Man's Dominion" is by no means a novel to be thrust aside as exhausted at one perusal.'—*Dundee Advertiser.*

Richard Pryce. WINIFRED MOUNT. By RICHARD PRYCE. *Second Edition. Crown 8vo. 3s. 6d.*

The 'Sussex Daily News' called this book '*a delightful story,*' and said that the writing was '*uniformly bright and graceful.*' The 'Daily Telegraph' said that the author was a '*deft and elegant story-teller,*' and that the book was '*an extremely clever story, utterly untainted by pessimism or vulgarity.*'

History

Gibbon. THE DECLINE AND FALL OF THE ROMAN EMPIRE. By EDWARD GIBBON. A New Edition, edited with Notes and Appendices and Maps by J. B. BURY, M.A., Fellow of Trinity College, Dublin. *In Seven Volumes. Crown 8vo.*

The time seems to have arrived for a new edition of Gibbon's great work—furnished with such notes and appendices as may bring it up to the standard of recent historical research. Edited by a scholar who has made this period his special study, and issued in a convenient form and at a moderate price, this edition should fill an obvious void.

Horsburgh. THE CAMPAIGN OF WATERLOO. By E. L. S. HORSBURGH, M.A. With Plans. *Crown 8vo. 5s.*

This is a full account of the final struggle of Napoleon, and contains a careful study from a strategical point of view of the movements of the French and allied armies.

George. BATTLES OF ENGLISH HISTORY. By H. B. GEORGE, M.A., Fellow of New College, Oxford. *With numerous Plans. Crown 8vo. 6s.*

This book, by a well-known authority on military history, will be an important contribution to the literature of the subject. All the great battles of English history are fully described, and connecting chapters carefully treat of the changes wrought by new discoveries and developments.

Oscar Browning. THE AGE OF THE CONDOTTIERI: A Short History of Italy from 1409 to 1530. By OSCAR BROWNING, M.A., Fellow of King's College, Cambridge. *Crown 8vo.* 5s.

This book is a continuation of Mr. Browning's 'Guelphs and Ghibellines,' and the two works form a complete account of Italian history from 1250 to 1530.

Biography

Southey. ENGLISH SEAMEN (Howard, Clifford, Hawkins, Drake, Cavendish). By ROBERT SOUTHEY. Edited, with an Introduction, by DAVID HANNAY. *Crown 8vo.* 6s.

This is a reprint of some excellent biographies of Elizabethan seamen, written by Southey and never republished. They are practically unknown, and they deserve, and will probably obtain, a wide popularity.

Cutts. AUGUSTINE OF CANTERBURY. By E. L. CUTTS, D.D. *Crown 8vo.* 3s. 6d.   [*Leaders of Religion.*

A biography of the first Archbishop of Canterbury, containing a fairly full account of the conversion of England.

Hutton. WILLIAM LAUD, ARCHBISHOP OF CANTERBURY: A Biography. By W. H. HUTTON, M.A., Fellow and and Tutor of St. John's College, Oxford. *Crown 8vo.* 3s. 6d.
[*Leaders of Religion.*

Mr. Hutton has made a special study of the life and times of Laud, and as the guardian of the Laudian relics and MSS. at Oxford, has been able to throw new light on various episodes in his career.

Mrs. Oliphant. THOMAS CHALMERS. By Mrs. OLIPHANT. *With a Portrait. Second Edition. Crown 8vo.* 3s. 6d.
[*Leaders of Religion.*

Lock. JOHN KEBLE. By WALTER LOCK, Sub-Warden of Keble College. *With a Portrait. Seventh Edition. Crown 8vo.* 3s. 6d.   [*Leaders of Religion.*

General Literature

Flinders Petrie. EGYPTIAN DECORATIVE ART. By W. M. FLINDERS PETRIE, D.C.L. With 120 Illustrations. *Crown 8vo.* 3s. 6d.

A book which deals with a subject which has never yet been seriously treated.

Flinders Petrie. EGYPTIAN TALES. Edited by W. M. FLINDERS PETRIE. Illustrated by TRISTRAM ELLIS. *Crown 8vo.* 3*s.* 6*d.*

A selection of the ancient tales of Egypt, edited from original sources, and of great importance as illustrating the life and society of ancient Egypt.

Ouida. ESSAYS by OUIDA. *Crown 8vo.* 6*s.*

This volume contains the following articles :—

Vulgarity.	The New Woman.
O Beati Insipientes!	Death and Pity.
Cities of Italy.	Conscription.
The Failure of Christianity.	Shelley.
The Sins of Society.	Some Fallacies of Science.
The Passing of Philomel.	Female Suffrage.
The Italy of To-day.	Gardens.
The Blind Guides of Italy.	The State as an Immoral Factor.
L'Uomo Fatale.	The Penalties of a Well-Known Name.

Oliphant. THE FRENCH RIVIERA. By Mrs. OLIPHANT and F. R. OLIPHANT. With Illustrations and Maps. *Crown 8vo.* 6*s.*

A volume dealing with the French Riviera from Toulon to Mentone. Without falling within the guide-book category, the book will supply some useful practical information, while occupying itself chiefly with descriptive and historical matter. A special feature will be the attention directed to those portions of the Riviera, which, though full of interest and easily accessible from many well-frequented spots, are generally left unvisited by English travellers, such as the Maures Mountains and the St. Tropez district, the country lying between Cannes, Grasse and the Var, and the magnificent valleys behind Nice. There will be several original illustrations.

Shedlock. THE PIANOFORTE SONATA: Its Origin and Development. By J. S. SHEDLOCK. *Crown 8vo.* 5*s.*

This is a practical and not unduly technical account of the Sonata treated historically. It contains several novel features, and an account of various works little known to the English public.

Dixon. A PRIMER OF TENNYSON. By W. M. DIXON, M.A., Professor of English Literature at Mason College. *Fcap. 8vo.* 1*s.* 6*d.*

This book consists of (1) a succinct but complete biography of Lord Tennyson; (2) an account of the volumes published by him in chronological order, dealing with the more important poems separately; (3) a concise criticism of Tennyson in his various aspects as lyrist, dramatist, and representative poet of his day; (4) a bibliography. Such a complete book on such a subject, and at such a moderate price, should find a host of readers.

THE CHRISTIAN YEAR. By JOHN KEBLE. With an Introduction and Notes by W LOCK, M.A., Sub-Warden of Keble College, Author of 'The Life of John Keble.' Illustrated by R. ANNING BELL. *Fcap. 8vo.* 3*s.* 6*d.*

A charming edition of a famous book, finely illustrated and printed in black and red, uniform with the 'Imitation of Christ.'

Theobald. INSECT LIFE. By F. W. THEOBALD, M.A. *Illustrated. Crown 8vo.* 2*s.* 6*d.* [*Univ. Extension Series.*

English Classics

Edited by W. E. HENLEY.

Messrs. Methuen propose to publish, under this title, a series of the masterpieces of the English tongue, which, while well within the reach of the average buyer, shall be at once an ornament to the shelf of him that owns, and a delight to the eye of him that reads.

The series, of which Mr. William Ernest Henley is the general editor, will confine itself to no single period or department of literature. Poetry, fiction, drama, biography, autobiography, letters, essays—in all these fields is the material of many goodly volumes.

The books, which are designed and printed by Messrs. Constable, will be issued in two editions—(1) A small edition, on the finest Japanese vellum, demy 8vo, 21*s.* a volume nett; (2) The popular edition on laid paper, crown 8vo, buckram, 3*s.* 6*d.* a volume.

The following are some notices which have appeared on 'TRISTRAM SHANDY,' the first volume of the series :—

'Very dainty volumes are these; the paper, type, and light green binding are all very agreeable to the eye. "Simplex munditiis" is the phrase that might be applied to them. So far as we know, Sterne's famous work has never appeared in a guise more attractive to the connoisseur than this.'—*Globe.*

'The book is excellently printed by Messrs. Constable on good paper, and being divided into two volumes, is light and handy without lacking the dignity of a classic.'—*Manchester Guardian.*

'This new edition of a great classic might make an honourable appearance in any library in the world. Printed by Constable on laid paper, bound in most artistic and restful-looking fig-green buckram, with a frontispiece portrait and an introduction by Mr. Charles Whibley, the book might well be issued at three times its present price.'—*Irish Independent.*

'Cheap and comely; a very agreeable edition.'—*Saturday Review.*

'A real acquisition to the library.'—*Birmingham Post.*

THE COMEDIES OF WILLIAM CONGREVE. With an Introduction by G. S. STREET, and a Portrait. 2 *vols.*

25 copies on Japanese paper.

THE LIVES OF DONNE, WOTTON, HOOKER, HERBERT, AND SANDERSON. By IZAAK WALTON. With an Introduction by VERNON BLACKBURN, and a Portrait.

25 copies on Japanese paper.

THE ADVENTURES OF HADJI BABA OF ISPAHAN. By JAMES MORIER. With an Introduction by E. S. BROWNE, M.A.

25 copies on Japanese paper.

THE POEMS OF ROBERT BURNS. With an Introduction by W. E. HENLEY, and a Portrait. 2 *vols.*

30 copies on Japanese paper.

THE LIVES OF THE ENGLISH POETS. By SAMUEL JOHNSON, LL.D. With an Introduction by JOHN HEPBURN MILLAR, and a Portrait. 3 *vols.*

30 copies on Japanese paper.

Classical Translations

NEW VOLUMES

Crown 8vo. Finely printed and bound in blue buckram.

SOPHOCLES—Electra and Ajax. Translated by E. D. A. MORSHEAD, M.A., late Scholar of New College, Oxford; Assistant Master at Winchester. 2*s.* 6*d.*

TACITUS—Agricola and Germania. Translated by R. B. TOWNSHEND, late Scholar of Trinity College, Cambridge. 2*s.* 6*d.*

𝔑𝔢𝔴 𝔞𝔫𝔡 𝔯𝔢𝔠𝔢𝔫𝔱 𝔅𝔬𝔬𝔨𝔰

Poetry

Rudyard Kipling. BARRACK-ROOM BALLADS; And Other Verses. By RUDYARD KIPLING. *Seventh Edition. Crown 8vo. 6s.*

A Special Presentation Edition, bound in white buckram, with extra gilt ornament. *7s. 6d.*

'Mr. Kipling's verse is strong, vivid, full of character. . . . Unmistakable genius rings in every line.'—*Times*.

'The disreputable lingo of Cockayne is henceforth justified before the world; for a man of genius has taken it in hand, and has shown, beyond all cavilling, that in its way it also is a medium for literature. You are grateful, and you say to yourself, half in envy and half in admiration: " Here is a *book*; here, or one is a Dutchman, is one of the books of the year." '—*National Observer*.

'"Barrack-Room Ballads" contains some of the best work that Mr. Kipling has ever done, which is saying a good deal. " Fuzzy-Wuzzy," "Gunga Din," and "Tommy," are, in our opinion, altogether superior to anything of the kind that English literature has hitherto produced.'—*Athenæum*.

'These ballads are as wonderful in their descriptive power as they are vigorous in their dramatic force. There are few ballads in the English language more stirring than "The Ballad of East and West," worthy to stand by the Border ballads of Scott.'—*Spectator*.

'The ballads teem with imagination, they palpitate with emotion. We read them with laughter and tears; the metres throb in our pulses, the cunningly ordered words tingle with life; and if this be not poetry, what is?'—*Pall Mall Gazette*.

Henley. LYRA HEROICA: An Anthology selected from the best English Verse of the 16th, 17th, 18th, and 19th Centuries. By WILLIAM ERNEST HENLEY, Author of 'A Book of Verse,' 'Views and Reviews,' etc. *Crown 8vo. Stamped gilt buckram, gilt top, edges uncut. 6s.*

'Mr. Henley has brought to the task of selection an instinct alike for poetry and for chivalry which seems to us quite wonderfully, and even unerringly, right.'—*Guardian*.

Jane Barlow. THE BATTLE OF THE FROGS AND MICE, translated by JANE BARLOW, Author of 'Irish Idylls,' and pictured by F. D. BEDFORD. *Small 4to. 6s. net.*

This is a new version of a famous old fable. Miss Barlow, whose brilliant volume of 'Irish Idylls' has gained her a wide reputation, has told the story in spirited flowing verse, and Mr. Bedford's numerous illustrations and ornaments are as spirited as the verse they picture.

Tomson. A SUMMER NIGHT, AND OTHER POEMS. By GRAHAM R. TOMSON. With Frontispiece by A. TOMSON. *Fcap. 8vo. 3s. 6d.*

An edition on hand-made paper, limited to 50 copies. *10s. 6d. net.*

'Mrs. Tomson holds perhaps the very highest rank among poetesses of English birth. This selection will help her reputation.'—*Black and White.*

Ibsen. BRAND. A Drama by HENRIK IBSEN. Translated by WILLIAM WILSON. *Crown 8vo. Second Edition. 3s. 6d.*

'The greatest world-poem of the nineteenth century next to "Faust." "Brand" will have an astonishing interest for Englishmen. It is in the same set with "Agamemnon," with "Lear," with the literature that we now instinctively regard as high and holy.'—*Daily Chronicle.*

"Q." GREEN BAYS: Verses and Parodies. By "Q.," Author of 'Dead Man's Rock,' etc. *Second Edition. Fcap. 8vo. 3s. 6d.*

'The verses display a rare and versatile gift of parody, great command of metre, and a very pretty turn of humour.'—*Times.*

"A. G." VERSES TO ORDER. By "A. G." *Cr. 8vo. 2s. 6d. net.*

A small volume of verse by a writer whose initials are well known to Oxford men.
'A capital specimen of light academic poetry. These verses are very bright and engaging, easy and sufficiently witty.'—*St. James's Gazette.*

Hosken. VERSES BY THE WAY. By J. D. HOSKEN. *Crown 8vo. 5s.*

A small edition on hand-made paper. *Price 12s. 6d. net.*

A Volume of Lyrics and Sonnets by J. D. Hosken, the Postman Poet. Q, the Author of 'The Splendid Spur,' writes a critical and biographical introduction.

Gale. CRICKET SONGS. By NORMAN GALE. *Crown 8vo. Linen. 2s. 6d.*

Also a limited edition on hand-made paper. *Demy 8vo. 10s. 6d. net.*

'They are wrung out of the excitement of the moment, and palpitate with the spirit of the game.'—*Star.*
'As healthy as they are spirited, and ought to have a great success.'—*Times.*
'Simple, manly, and humorous. Every cricketer should buy the book.'—*Westminster Gazette.* 'Cricket has never known such a singer.'—*Cricket.*

Langbridge. BALLADS OF THE BRAVE: Poems of Chivalry, Enterprise, Courage, and Constancy, from the Earliest Times to the Present Day. Edited, with Notes, by Rev. F. LANGBRIDGE. *Crown 8vo. Buckram 3s. 6d.* School Edition, *2s. 6d.*

'A very happy conception happily carried out. These "Ballads of the Brave" are intended to suit the real tastes of boys, and will suit the taste of the great majority.' —*Spectator.* 'The book is full of splendid things.'—*World.*

English Classics

Edited by W. E. HENLEY.

Messrs. Methuen are publishing, under this title, a series of the masterpieces of the English tongue, which, while well within the reach of the average buyer, shall be at once an ornament to the shelf of him that owns, and a delight to the eye of him that reads.

The series, of which Mr. William Ernest Henley is the general editor, will confine itself to no single period or department of literature. Poetry, fiction, drama, biography, autobiography, letters, essays—in all these fields is the material of many goodly volumes.

The books, which are designed and printed by Messrs. Constable, are issued in two editions—(1) A small edition, on the finest Japanese vellum, demy 8vo, 21s. a volume nett; (2) the popular edition on laid paper, crown 8vo, 3s. 6d. a volume.

THE LIFE AND OPINIONS OF TRISTRAM SHANDY.

By LAWRENCE STERNE. With an Introduction by CHARLES WHIBLEY, and a Portrait. *2 vols. 7s.*

60 copies on Japanese paper. *42s.*

'Very dainty volumes are these; the paper, type and light green binding are all very agreeable to the eye. "Simplex munditiis" is the phrase that might be applied to them. So far as we know, Sterne's famous work has never appeared in a guise more attractive to the connoisseur than this.'—*Globe.*

'The book is excellently printed by Messrs. Constable on good paper, and being divided into two volumes, is light and handy without lacking the dignity of a classic.'—*Manchester Guardian.*

'This new edition of a great classic might make an honourable appearance in any library in the world. Printed by Constable on laid paper, bound in most artistic and restful-looking fig-green buckram, with a frontispiece portrait and an introduction by Mr. Charles Whibley, the book might well be issued at three times its present price.'—*Irish Independent.*

'Cheap and comely; a very agreeable edition.'—*Saturday Review.*

'A real acquisition to the library.'—*Birmingham Post.*

History

Flinders Petrie. A HISTORY OF EGYPT, FROM THE EARLIEST TIMES TO THE HYKSOS. By W. M. FLINDERS PETRIE, D.C.L., Professor of Egyptology at University College. *Fully Illustrated. Crown 8vo. 6s.*

'An important contribution to scientific study.'—*Scotsman.*

'A history written in the spirit of scientific precision so worthily represented by Dr. Petrie and his school cannot but promote sound and accurate study, and supply a vacant place in the English literature of Egyptology.'—*Times.*

Flinders Petrie. TELL EL AMARNA. By W. M. FLINDERS PETRIE, D.C.L. With chapters by Professor A. H. SAYCE, D.D.; F. LL. GRIFFITH, F.S.A.; and F. C. J. SPURRELL, F.G.S. With numerous coloured illustrations. *Royal 4to. 20s. net.*

Clark. THE COLLEGES OF OXFORD : Their History and their Traditions. By Members of the University. Edited by A. CLARK, M.A., Fellow and Tutor of Lincoln College. *8vo.* 12s. 6d.

'Whether the reader approaches the book as a patriotic member of a college, as an antiquary, or as a student of the organic growth of college foundation, it will amply reward his attention.'—*Times.*

' A delightful book, learned and lively.'—*Academy.*

' A work which will certainly be appealed to for many years as the standard book on the Colleges of Oxford.'—*Athenæum.*

Perrens. THE HISTORY OF FLORENCE FROM THE TIME OF THE MEDICIS TO THE FALL OF THE REPUBLIC. By F. T. PERRENS. Translated by HANNAH LYNCH. *In Three Volumes. Vol. I. 8vo.* 12s. 6d.

This is a translation from the French of the best history of Florence in existence. This volume covers a period of profound interest—political and literary—and is written with great vivacity.

' This is a standard book by an honest and intelligent historian, who has deserved well of his countrymen, and of all who are interested in Italian history.'—*Manchester Guardian.*

Browning. GUELPHS AND GHIBELLINES: A Short History of Mediæval Italy, A.D. 1250-1409. By OSCAR BROWNING, Fellow and Tutor of King's College, Cambridge. *Second Edition. Crown 8vo.* 5s.

'A very able book.'—*Westminster Gazette.*

'A vivid picture of mediæval Italy.'—*Standard.*

O'Grady. THE STORY OF IRELAND. By STANDISH O'GRADY, Author of ' Finn and his Companions.' *Cr. 8vo.* 2s. 6d.

' Novel and very fascinating history. Wonderfully alluring.'—*Cork Examiner.*

'Most delightful, most stimulating. Its racy humour, its original imaginings, its perfectly unique history, make it one of the freshest, breeziest volumes.'—*Methodist Times.*

'A survey at once graphic, acute, and quaintly written.'—*Times.*

Malden. ENGLISH RECORDS. A Companion to the History of England. By H. E. MALDEN, M.A. *Crown 8vo.* 3s. 6d.

A book which aims at concentrating information upon dates, genealogy, officials, constitutional documents, etc., which is usually found scattered in different volumes.

Biography

Collingwood. JOHN RUSKIN : His Life and Work. By W. G. COLLINGWOOD, M.A., Editor of Mr. Ruskin's Poems. *2 vols. 8vo.* 32s. *Second Edition.*

This important work is written by Mr. Collingwood, who has been for some years Mr. Ruskin's private secretary, and who has had unique advantages in obtaining materials for this book from Mr. Ruskin himself and from his friends. It contains a large amount of new matter, and of letters which have never been published, and is, in fact, a full and authoritative biography of Mr. Ruskin. The book contains numerous portraits of Mr. Ruskin including a coloured one from a water-colour portrait by himself, and also 13 sketches, never before published, by Mr. Ruskin and Mr. Arthur Severn. A bibliography is added.

'No more magnificent volumes have been published for a long time. . . .'—*Times.*

'This most lovingly written and most profoundly interesting book.'—*Daily News.*

'It is long since we have had a biography with such varied delights of substance and of form. Such a book is a pleasure for the day, and a joy for ever.'—*Daily Chronicle.*

'Mr. Ruskin could not well have been more fortunate in his biographer.'—*Globe.*

'A noble monument of a noble subject. One of the most beautiful books about one of the noblest lives of our century.'—*Glasgow Herald.*

Waldstein. JOHN RUSKIN : a Study. By CHARLES WALD-STEIN, M.A., Fellow of King's College, Cambridge. With a Photogravure Portrait after Professor HERKOMER. *Post 8vo.* 5s.

Also 25 copies on Japanese paper. *Demy 8vo.* 21s.

'Ruskinites will no doubt arise and join battle with Mr. Waldstein, who, all the same has produced a remarkably fine piece of criticism, which is well worth reading for its own sake.'—*Glasgow Herald.*

'A thoughtful, impartial, well-written criticism of Ruskin's teaching, intended to separate what the author regards as valuable and permanent from what is transient and erroneous in the great master's writing.'—*Daily Chronicle.*

Robbins. THE EARLY LIFE OF WILLIAM EWART GLADSTONE. By A. F. ROBBINS. *With Portraits. Crown 8vo.* 6s.

'The earlier years of Mr. Gladstone's political life stand out all the more finely, and leave a more enduring impression, because of the absolute truthfulness and conscientiousness with which the record has been penned.'—*Glasgow Herald.*

'Considerable labour and much skill of presentation have not been unworthily expended on this interesting work.'—*Times.*

'By immense labour, guided by a competent knowledge of affairs, he has given us a book which will be of permanent value to the student of political history. It is exhaustively indexed, and accompanied by three portraits.'—*Yorkshire Post.*

'Not only one of the most meritorious, but one of the most interesting, biographical works that have appeared on the subject of the ex-Premier. . . . It furnishes a picture from many points original and striking ; it makes additions of value to the evidence on which we are entitled to estimate a great public character ; and it gives the reader's judgment exactly that degree of guidance which is the function of a calm, restrained, and judicious historian.'—*Birmingham Daily Post.*

'A carefully-planned narrative, into which is woven a great deal of information. . . . It is pretty safe to predict that this volume will not only be read but retained on library bookshelves as a useful book of reference.'—*Daily News.*

Clark Russell. THE LIFE OF ADMIRAL LORD COL-LINGWOOD. By W. CLARK RUSSELL, Author of 'The Wreck of the Grosvenor.' With Illustrations by F. BRANGWYN. *Second Edition. Crown 8vo.* 6s.

'A really good book.'—*Saturday Review.*

'A most excellent and wholesome book, which we should like to see in the hands of every boy in the country.'—*St. James's Gazette.*

General Literature

Gladstone. THE SPEECHES AND PUBLIC ADDRESSES
OF THE RT. HON. W. E. GLADSTONE, M.P. With Notes
and Introductions. Edited by A. W. HUTTON, M.A. (Librarian of
the Gladstone Library), and H. J. COHEN, M.A. With Portraits.
8vo. Vols. IX. and X. 12s. 6d. each.

Henley and Whibley. A BOOK OF ENGLISH PROSE.
Collected by W. E. HENLEY and CHARLES WHIBLEY. *Cr. 8vo. 6s.*
Also 40 copies on Dutch paper. *21s. net.*
Also 15 copies on Japanese paper. *42s. net.*

'A unique volume of extracts—an art gallery of early prose.'—*Birmingham Post.*
'The book is delightfully got up, being printed by Messrs. Constable, who have
  evidently bestowed most loving care upon it.'—*Publishers' Circular.*
'The anthology is one every lover of good writing and quaint English will enjoy.'—
  Literary World.
'An admirable companion to Mr. Henley's "Lyra Heroica."'—*Saturday Review.*
'Quite delightful. The choice made has been excellent, and the volume has been
  most admirably printed by Messrs. Constable. A greater treat for those not well
  acquainted with pre-Restoration prose could not be imagined.'—*Athenæum.*

Wells. OXFORD AND OXFORD LIFE. By Members of
the University. Edited by J. WELLS, M.A., Fellow and Tutor of
Wadham College. *Crown 8vo. 3s. 6d.*

This work contains an account of life at Oxford—intellectual, social, and religious—
  a careful estimate of necessary expenses, a review of recent changes, a statement
  of the present position of the University, and chapters on Women's Education,
  aids to study, and University Extension.
'We congratulate Mr. Wells on the production of a readable and intelligent account
  of Oxford as it is at the present time, written by persons who are, with hardly an
  exception, possessed of a close acquaintance with the system and life of the
  University.'—*Athenæum.*

Chalmers Mitchell. OUTLINES OF BIOLOGY. By P.
CHALMERS MITCHELL, M.A., F.Z.S. *Fully Illustrated. Crown
8vo. 6s.*

A text-book designed to cover the new Schedule issued by the Royal College of
  Physicians and Surgeons.

Dixon. ENGLISH POETRY FROM BLAKE TO BROWN-
ING. By W. M. DIXON, M.A. *Crown 8vo. 3s. 6d.*

A Popular Account of the poetry of the Century.
'Scholarly in conception, and full of sound and suggestive criticism.'—*Times.*
'The book is remarkable for freshness of thought expressed in graceful language.'—
  Manchester Examiner.

Bowden. THE EXAMPLE OF BUDDHA: Being Quota-
tions from Buddhist Literature for each Day in the Year. Compiled
by E. M. BOWDEN. With Preface by Sir EDWIN ARNOLD. *Third
Edition. 16mo. 2s. 6d.*

Massee. A MONOGRAPH OF THE MYXOGASTRES. By
GEORGE MASSEE. With 12 Coloured Plates. *Royal 8vo.* 18s. *net.*
'A work much in advance of any book in the language treating of this group of
organisms. It is indispensable to every student of the Myxogastres. The
coloured plates deserve high praise for their accuracy and execution.'—*Nature.*

Bushill. PROFIT SHARING AND THE LABOUR QUES-
TION. By T. W. BUSHILL, a Profit Sharing Employer. With an
Introduction by SEDLEY TAYLOR, Author of 'Profit Sharing between
Capital and Labour.' *Crown 8vo.* 2s. 6d.

Jenks. ENGLISH LOCAL GOVERNMENT. By E JENKS,
M.A., Professor of Law at University College, Liverpool. *Crown
8vo.* 2s. 6d.
'The work is admirably done. Everything the average man will wish to know
respecting the history and hearing of the subject he is likely to learn from Professor
Jenks. He is told something of the origin of every form of the government under
which he lives and is rated, and may learn sufficient of the duties and powers of
local bodies to enable him to take an intelligent interest in their work.'—*Western
Morning News.*
'Timely and admirable.'—*Scotsman.*
'Mr. Jenks undertakes to give in a brief compass an accurate description of the
public bodies and authorities by which we are surrounded, while just glancing
here and there at their origin and historical continuity through the ages. A
subject of much complexity is here judiciously summarised.'—*Daily News.*
'We can cordially recommend the book as giving an excellent outline in general
terms of English local government.'—*School Guardian.*

Malden. THE ENGLISH CITIZEN: HIS RIGHTS AND
DUTIES. By H. E. MALDEN, M.A. *Crown 8vo.* 1s. 6d.
A simple account of the privileges and duties of the English citizen.

John Beever. PRACTICAL FLY-FISHING, Founded on
Nature, by JOHN BEEVER, late of the Thwaite House, Coniston. A
New Edition, with a Memoir of the Author by W. G. COLLINGWOOD,
M.A. Also additional Notes and a chapter on Char-Fishing, by A.
and A. R. SEVERN. With a specially designed title-page. *Crown
8vo.* 3s. 6d.
A little book on Fly-Fishing by an old friend of Mr. Ruskin. It has been out of
print for some time, and being still much in request, is now issued with a Memoir
of the Author by W. G. Collingwood.

Hutton. THE VACCINATION QUESTION. A Letter to
the Right Hon. H. H. ASQUITH, M.P. By A. W. HUTTON,
M.A. *Crown 8vo.* 1s. 6d.

Theology

Driver. SERMONS ON SUBJECTS CONNECTED WITH THE OLD TESTAMENT. By S. R. DRIVER, D.D., Canon of Christ Church, Regius Professor of Hebrew in the University of Oxford. *Crown 8vo.* 6s.

'A welcome companion to the author's famous 'Introduction.' No man can read these discourses without feeling that Dr. Driver is fully alive to the deeper teaching of the Old Testament.'—*Guardian.*

Cheyne. FOUNDERS OF OLD TESTAMENT CRITICISM: Biographical, Descriptive, and Critical Studies. By T. K. CHEYNE, D.D., Oriel Professor of the Interpretation of Holy Scripture at Oxford. *Large crown 8vo.* 7s. 6d.

This important book is a historical sketch of O.T. Criticism in the form of biographical studies from the days of Eichhorn to those of Driver and Robertson Smith. It is the only book of its kind in English.
'The volume is one of great interest and value. It displays all the author's well-known ability and learning, and its opportune publication has laid all students of theology, and specially of Bible criticism, under weighty obligation.'—*Scotsman.*
'A very learned and instructive work.'—*Times.*

Prior. CAMBRIDGE SERMONS. Edited by C. H. PRIOR, M.A., Fellow and Tutor of Pembroke College. *Crown 8vo.* 6s.

A volume of sermons preached before the University of Cambridge by various preachers, including the Archbishop of Canterbury and Bishop Westcott.
'A representative collection. Bishop Westcott's is a noble sermon.'—*Guardian.*
'Full of thoughtfulness and dignity.'—*Record.*

Beeching. SERMONS TO SCHOOLBOYS. By H. C. BEECHING, M.A., Rector of Yattendon, Berks. With a Preface by CANON SCOTT HOLLAND. *Crown 8vo.* 2s. 6d.

Seven sermons preached before the boys of Bradfield College.

Layard. RELIGION IN BOYHOOD. Notes on the Religious Training of Boys. With a Preface by J. R. ILLINGWORTH. By E. B. LAYARD, M.A. *18mo.* 1s.

James. CURIOSITIES OF CHRISTIAN HISTORY PRIOR TO THE REFORMATION. By CROAKE JAMES, Author of 'Curiosities of Law and Lawyers.' *Crown 8vo.* 7s. 6d.

'This volume contains a great deal of quaint and curious matter, affording some "particulars of the interesting persons, episodes, and events from the Christian's point of view during the first fourteen centuries." Wherever we dip into his pages we find something worth dipping into.'—*John Bull.*

Kaufmann. CHARLES KINGSLEY. By M. KAUFMANN, M.A. *Crown 8vo. Buckram.* 5s.

A biography of Kingsley, especially dealing with his achievements in social reform.
'The author has certainly gone about his work with conscientiousness and industry.'—*Sheffield Daily Telegraph.*

Devotional Books.
With Full-page Illustrations.

THE IMITATION OF CHRIST. By THOMAS À KEMPIS. With an Introduction by ARCHDEACON FARRAR. Illustrated by C. M. GERE, and printed in black and red. *Fcap. 8vo.* 3s. 6d.

'A new and beautiful edition of a book that will abide during the ages. The paging and type-work are perfect, and the effect is heightened by the large, fine-cut metal letter in vermilion which marks the beginning of each verse or paragraph of the volume.'—*Freeman's Journal.*

'We must draw attention to the antique style, quaintness, and typographical excellence of the work, its red-letter 'initials' and black letter type, and old-fashioned paragraphic arrangement of pages. The antique paper, uncut edges, and illustrations are in accord with the other features of this unique little work.'—*Newsagent.*

'Amongst all the innumerable English editions of the 'Imitation,' there can have been few which were prettier than this one, printed in strong and handsome type by Messrs. Constable, with all the glory of red initials, and the comfort of buckram binding.'—*Glasgow Herald.*

THE CHRISTIAN YEAR. By JOHN KEBLE. With an Introduction and Notes by W. LOCK, M.A., Sub-Warden of Keble College, Author of 'The Life of John Keble.' Illustrated by R. ANNING BELL. *Fcap. 8vo.* 5s.   [*Easter.*

Leaders of Religion

Edited by H. C. BEECHING, M.A. *With Portraits, crown 8vo.*

A series of short biographies of the most prominent leaders of religious life and thought of all ages and countries.

2/6 & 3/6

The following are ready—   2s. 6d.

CARDINAL NEWMAN. By R. H. HUTTON. *Second Edition.*

'Few who read this book will fail to be struck by the wonderful insight it displays into the nature of the Cardinal's genius and the spirit of his life.'—WILFRID WARD, in the *Tablet.*

'Full of knowledge, excellent in method, and intelligent in criticism. We regard it as wholly admirable.'—*Academy.*

JOHN WESLEY. By J. H. OVERTON, M.A.

'It is well done: the story is clearly told, proportion is duly observed, and there is no lack either of discrimination or of sympathy.'—*Manchester Guardian.*

BISHOP WILBERFORCE. By G. W. DANIEL, M.A.

CARDINAL MANNING. By A. W. HUTTON, M.A.

CHARLES SIMEON. By H. C. G. MOULE, M.A.

3s. 6d.

JOHN KEBLE. By WALTER LOCK, M.A. *Seventh Edition.*

THOMAS CHALMERS. By Mrs. OLIPHANT. *Second Edition.*

LANCELOT ANDREWES, Bishop of Winchester. By R. L. OTTLEY, M.A.

'A very interesting and skilful monograph.'—*Times.*
'Mr. Ottley has told the story of a great career with judgment and knowledge, and he has not forgotten to indicate either the forces which shaped it, or the force which it has in turn contributed to the shaping of the religious life of to-day.—*Leeds Mercury.*

AUGUSTINE OF CANTERBURY. By E. L. CUTTS, D.D.

WILLIAM LAUD. By W. H. HUTTON, M.A.

Other volumes will be announced in due course.

Works by S. Baring Gould

OLD COUNTRY LIFE. With Sixty-seven Illustrations by W. PARKINSON, F. D. BEDFORD, and F. MASEY. *Large Crown 8vo, cloth super extra, top edge gilt,* 10s. 6d. *Fifth and Cheaper Edition.* 6s.

'"Old Country Life," as healthy wholesome reading, full of breezy life and movement, full of quaint stories vigorously told, will not be excelled by any book to be published throughout the year. Sound, hearty, and English to the core.'—*World.*

HISTORIC ODDITIES AND STRANGE EVENTS. *Third Edition. Crown 8vo.* 6s.

'A collection of exciting and entertaining chapters. The whole volume is delightful reading.'—*Times.*

FREAKS OF FANATICISM. *Third Edition. Crown 8vo.* 6s.

'Mr. Baring Gould has a keen eye for colour and effect, and the subjects he has chosen give ample scope to his descriptive and analytic faculties. A perfectly fascinating book.'—*Scottish Leader.*

A GARLAND OF COUNTRY SONG: English Folk Songs with their traditional melodies. Collected and arranged by S. BARING GOULD and H. FLEETWOOD SHEPPARD. *Demy 4to.* 6s.

SONGS OF THE WEST: Traditional Ballads and Songs of the West of England, with their Traditional Melodies. Collected by S. BARING GOULD, M.A., and H. FLEETWOOD SHEPPARD, M.A. Arranged for Voice and Piano. In 4 Parts (containing 25 Songs each), *Parts I., II., III.,* 3s. *each. Part IV.,* 5s. *In one Vol., French morocco,* 15s.

'A rich and varied collection of humour, pathos, grace, and poetic fancy. —*Saturday Review.*

A BOOK OF FAIRY TALES retold by S. BARING GOULD
With numerous illustrations and initial letters by ARTHUR J. GASKIN.
Crown 8vo. Buckram. 6s.

'The stories are old friends—Cinderella, Bluebeard, the Three Bears, and so on—in a new dress of simple language which their skilled reviser has given them. They make a delightful collection, and Mr. Gaskin's illustrations have a beauty all their own, a beauty which some will judge to be beyond the appreciation of children, but a child is sure to be interested by these pictures, and the impression they give cannot but have the best effect in the formation of a good taste.'—*Scotsman.*

'Mr. Baring Gould has done a good deed, and is deserving of gratitude, in re-writing in honest, simple style the old stories that delighted the childhood of "our fathers and grandfathers." We do not think he has omitted any of our favourite stories, the stories that are commonly regarded as merely "old-fashioned." As to the form of the book, and the printing, which is by Messrs. Constable, it were difficult to commend overmuch.'—*Saturday Review.*

YORKSHIRE ODDITIES AND STRANGE EVENTS.
Fourth Edition. Crown 8vo. 6s.

STRANGE SURVIVALS AND SUPERSTITIONS. With
Illustrations. By S. BARING GOULD. *Crown 8vo. Second Edition.
6s.*

A book on such subjects as Foundations, Gables, Holes, Gallows, Raising the Hat, Old Ballads, etc. etc. It traces in a most interesting manner their origin and history.

'We have read Mr. Baring Gould's book from beginning to end. It is full of quaint and various information, and there is not a dull page in it.'—*Notes and Queries.*

THE TRAGEDY OF THE CAESARS: The
Emperors of the Julian and Claudian Lines. With numerous Illustrations from Busts, Gems, Cameos, etc. By S. BARING GOULD,
Author of 'Mehalah,' etc. *Third Edition. Royal 8vo. 15s.*

'A most splendid and fascinating book on a subject of undying interest. The great feature of the book is the use the author has made of the existing portraits of the Caesars, and the admirable critical subtlety he has exhibited in dealing with this line of research. It is brilliantly written, and the illustrations are supplied on a scale of profuse magnificence.'—*Daily Chronicle.*

'The volumes will in no sense disappoint the general reader. Indeed, in their way, there is nothing in any sense so good in English. . . . Mr. Baring Gould has presented his narrative in such a way as not to make one dull page.'—*Athenæum.*

THE DESERTS OF SOUTHERN FRANCE. By S. BARING
GOULD. With numerous Illustrations by F. D. BEDFORD, S.
HUTTON, etc. *2 vols. Demy 8vo. 32s.*

This book is the first serious attempt to describe the great barren tableland that extends to the south of Limousin in the Department of Aveyron, Lot, etc., a country of dolomite cliffs, and cañons, and subterranean rivers. The region is full of prehistoric and historic interest, relics of cave-dwellers, of mediæval robbers, and of the English domination and the Hundred Years' War.

'His two richly-illustrated volumes are full of matter of interest to the geologist, the archæologist, and the student of history and manners.'—*Scotsman.*

'It deals with its subject in a manner which rarely fails to arrest and enchain attention.'—*Times.*

'We leave the author with a clear and delightful knowledge of the district and with a fresh attraction towards himself.'—*Leeds Mercury.*

'A wholly original and singularly attractive work.'—*Daily News.*

MR. BARING GOULD'S NOVELS

'To say that a book is by the author of "Mehalah" is to imply that it contains a story cast on strong lines, containing dramatic possibilities, vivid and sympathetic descriptions of Nature, and a wealth of ingenious imagery.'—*Speaker.*

'That whatever Mr. Baring Gould writes is well worth reading, is a conclusion that may be very generally accepted. His views of life are fresh and vigorous, his language pointed and characteristic, the incidents of which he makes use are striking and original, his characters are life-like, and though somewhat exceptional people, are drawn and coloured with artistic force. Add to this that his descriptions of scenes and scenery are painted with the loving eyes and skilled hands of a master of his art, that he is always fresh and never dull, and under such conditions it is no wonder that readers have gained confidence both in his power of amusing and satisfying them, and that year by year his popularity widens.'—*Court Circular.*

SIX SHILLINGS EACH

IN THE ROAR OF THE SEA : A Tale of the Cornish Coast.

MRS. CURGENVEN OF CURGENVEN.

CHEAP JACK ZITA.

THE QUEEN OF LOVE.

KITTY ALONE.

THREE SHILLINGS AND SIXPENCE EACH

ARMINELL : A Social Romance.

URITH : A Story of Dartmoor.

MARGERY OF QUETHER, and other Stories.

JACQUETTA, and other Stories.

Fiction

SIX SHILLING NOVELS

Marie Corelli. BARABBAS : A DREAM OF THE WORLD'S TRAGEDY. By MARIE CORELLI, Author of ' A Romance of Two Worlds,' ' Vendetta,' etc. *Fourteenth Edition. Crown 8vo. 6s.*

'The tender reverence of the treatment and the imaginative beauty of the writing have reconciled us to the daring of the conception, and the conviction is forced on us that even so exalted a subject cannot be made too familiar to us, provided it be presented in the true spirit of Christian faith. The amplifications of the Scripture narrative are often conceived with high poetic insight, and this "Dream of the World's Tragedy" is, despite some trifling incongruities, a lofty and not inadequate paraphrase of the supreme climax of the inspired narrative.'—*Dublin Review.*

Anthony Hope. THE GOD IN THE CAR. By ANTHONY HOPE, Author of ' A Change of Air,' etc. *Sixth Edition. Crown 8vo. 6s.*

' "The God in the Car" is so good, so immeasurably better than anything Mr. Hope has done before in the way of a novel of contemporary manners, that there seems no reason why he should not eventually reach that place in the front rank, which he has evidently set before himself as his goal. "The God in the Car" is a novel eminently worth reading, full of brilliance, fire, and daring, and above all full of promise of something still better in the future, something which will render criticism superfluous.'—*Manchester Guardian*.

'Ruston is drawn with extraordinary skill, and Maggie Dennison with many subtle strokes. The minor characters are clear cut. In short the book is a brilliant one. "The God in the Car" is one of the most remarkable works in a year that has given us the handiwork of nearly all our best living novelists.'—*Standard*.

'A very remarkable book, deserving of critical analysis impossible within our limit; brilliant, but not superficial; well considered, but not elaborated; constructed with the proverbial art that conceals, but yet allows itself to be enjoyed by readers to whom fine literary method is a keen pleasure; true without cynicism, subtle without affectation, humorous without strain, witty without offence, inevitably sad, with an unmorose simplicity.'—*The World*.

Anthony Hope. A CHANGE OF AIR. By ANTHONY HOPE, Author of ' The Prisoner of Zenda,' etc. *Crown 8vo.* 6s.

'A graceful, vivacious comedy, true to human nature. The characters are traced with a masterly hand.'—*Times*.

Anthony Hope. A MAN OF MARK. By ANTHONY HOPE. Author of 'The Prisoner of Zenda,' 'The God in the Car,' etc. *Second Edition. Crown 8vo.* 6s.

This is a re-issue of Anthony Hope's first novel. It has been out of print for some years, and in view of the great popularity of the author, it has been reprinted. It is a story of political adventure in South America, and is rather in the style of ' The Prisoner of Zenda.'

Conan Doyle. ROUND THE RED LAMP. By A. CONAN DOYLE, Author of 'The White Company,' 'The Adventures of Sherlock Holmes,' etc. *Third Edition. Crown 8vo.* 6s.

'The reader will find in it some perfectly constructed stories, the memory of which will haunt him long after he has laid it down. The author again reveals himself as a keenly sympathetic observer of life and a master of vigorous impressive narrative.'—*Yorkshire Post*.

'The book is, indeed, composed of leaves from life, and is far and away the best view that has been vouchsafed us behind the scenes of the consulting-room. It is very superior to "The Diary of a late Physician."'—*Illustrated London News*.

'Dr. Doyle wields a cunning pen, as all the world now knows. His deft touch is seen to perfection in these short sketches—these "facts and fancies of medical life," as he calls them. Every page reveals the literary artist, the keen observer, the trained delineator of human nature, its weal and its woe.'—*Freeman's Journal*.

'These tales are skilful, attractive, and eminently suited to give relief to the mind of a reader in quest of distraction.'—*Athenæum*.

'The book is one to buy as well as to borrow, and that it will repay both buyer and borrower with interest.'—*Sunday Times*.

'It is quite safe to assert that no one who begins to read 'Round the Red Lamp' will voluntarily lay the book aside until every one of its fascinating pages has been perused.'—*Lady*.

'No more interesting and occasionally sensational stories have appeared than these.'—*Punch*.

Stanley Weyman. UNDER THE RED ROBE. By STANLEY
WEYMAN, Author of 'A Gentleman of France.' With Twelve Illustrations by R. Caton Woodville. *Sixth Edition.* *Crown 8vo.* 6s.

A cheaper edition of a book which won instant popularity. No unfavourable review
occurred, and most critics spoke in terms of enthusiastic admiration. The 'Westminster Gazette' called it '*a book of which we have read every word for the sheer
pleasure of reading, and which we put down with a pang that we cannot forget
it all and start again.*' The 'Daily Chronicle' said that '*every one who reads
books at all must read this thrilling romance, from the first page of which to the
last the breathless reader is haled along.*' It also called the book '*an inspiration
of manliness and courage.*' The 'Globe' called it '*a delightful tale of chivalry
and adventure, vivid and dramatic, with a wholesome modesty and reverence
for the highest.*'

E. F. Benson. DODO: A DETAIL OF THE DAY. By E. F.
BENSON. *Crown 8vo.* *Fourteenth Edition.* 6s.

A story of society which attracted by its brilliance universal attention. The best
critics were cordial in their praise. The 'Guardian' spoke of 'Dodo' as '*unusually clever and interesting*'; the 'Spectator' called it '*a delightfully witty
sketch of society*;' the 'Speaker' said the dialogue was '*a perpetual feast of
epigram and paradox*'; the 'Athenæum' spoke of the author as '*a writer
of quite exceptional ability*'; the 'Academy' praised his '*amazing cleverness*;'
the 'World' said the book was '*brilliantly written*'; and half-a-dozen papers
declared there was '*not a dull page in the book.*'

E. F. Benson. THE RUBICON. By E. F. BENSON, Author of
'Dodo.' *Fourth Edition.* *Crown 8vo.* 6s.

Of Mr. Benson's second novel the 'Birmingham Post' says it is '*well written,
stimulating, unconventional, and, in a word, characteristic*': the 'National
Observer' congratulates Mr. Benson upon '*an exceptional achievement,*' and
calls the book '*a notable advance on his previous work.*'

Baring Gould. IN THE ROAR OF THE SEA: A Tale of
the Cornish Coast. By S. BARING GOULD. *Fifth Edition.* 6s.

Baring Gould. MRS. CURGENVEN OF CURGENVEN.
By S. BARING GOULD. *Third Edition.* 6s.

A story of Devon life. The 'Graphic' speaks of it as '*a novel of vigorous humour and
sustained power*'; the 'Sussex Daily News' says that '*the swing of the narrative
is splendid*'; and the 'Speaker' mentions its '*bright imaginative power.*'

Baring Gould. CHEAP JACK ZITA. By S. BARING GOULD.
Third Edition. *Crown 8vo.* 6s.

A Romance of the Ely Fen District in 1815, which the 'Westminster Gazette' calls
'*a powerful drama of human passion*'; and the 'National Observer' '*a story
worthy the author.*'

Baring Gould. THE QUEEN OF LOVE. By S. BARING
GOULD. *Second Edition.* *Crown 8vo.* 6s.

The 'Glasgow Herald' says that '*the scenery is admirable, and the dramatic incidents are most striking.*' The 'Westminster Gazette' calls the book '*strong,
interesting, and clever.*' 'Punch' says that '*you cannot put it down until you
have finished it.*' 'The Sussex Daily News' says that it '*can be heartily recommended to all who care for cleanly, energetic, and interesting fiction.*'

Baring Gould. KITTY ALONE. By S. BARING GOULD, Author of 'Mehalah,' 'Cheap Jack Zita,' etc. *Second Edition. Crown 8vo. 6s.*

'A strong and original story, teeming with graphic description, stirring incident, and, above all, with vivid and enthralling human interest.'—*Daily Telegraph.*

'Brisk, clever, keen, healthy, humorous, and interesting.'—*National Observer.*

'Full of quaint and delightful studies of character.'—*Bristol Mercury.*

W. E. Norris. MATTHEW AUSTIN. By W. E. NORRIS, Author of ' Mdlle. de Mersac,' etc. *Second Edition. Crown 8vo. 6s.*

' "Matthew Austin" may safely be pronounced one of the most intellectually satisfactory and morally bracing novels of the current year.'—*Daily Telegraph.*

'The characters are carefully and cleverly drawn, and the story is ingenious and interesting.'—*Guardian.*

'Mr. W. E. Norris is always happy in his delineation of every-day experiences, but rarely has he been brighter or breezier than in "Matthew Austin." The pictures are in Mr. Norris's pleasantest vein, while running through the entire story is a felicity of style and wholesomeness of tone which one is accustomed to find in the novels of this favourite author.'—*Scotsman.*

'Mr. Norris writes as an educated and shrewd observer, and as a gentleman.'— *Pall Mall Budget.*

W. E. Norris. HIS GRACE. By W. E. NORRIS, Author of ' Mademoiselle de Mersac.' *Third Edition. Crown 8vo. 6s.*

'The characters are delineated by the author with his characteristic skill and vivacity, and the story is told with that ease of manners and Thackerayean insight which give strength of flavour to Mr. Norris's novels No one can depict the Englishwoman of the better classes with more subtlety.'—*Glasgow Herald.*

'Mr. Norris has drawn a really fine character in the Duke of Hurstbourne, at once unconventional and very true to the conventionalities of life, weak and strong in a breath, capable of inane follies and heroic decisions, yet not so definitely portrayed as to relieve a reader of the necessity of study on his own behalf.'— *Athenæum.*

Gilbert Parker. MRS. FALCHION. By GILBERT PARKER, Author of ' Pierre and His People.' *New Edition. 6s.*

Mr. Parker's second book has received a warm welcome. The 'Athenæum' called it ' *a splendid study of character* '; the ' Pall Mall Gazette ' spoke of the writing as ' *but little behind anything that has been done by any writer of our time* '; the ' St. James's ' called it ' *a very striking and admirable novel* '; and the ' Westminster Gazette ' applied to it the epithet of ' *distinguished.* '

Gilbert Parker. PIERRE AND HIS PEOPLE. By GILBERT PARKER. *Crown 8vo. Buckram. 6s.*

'Stories happily conceived and finely executed. There is strength and genius in Mr. Parker's style.'—*Daily Telegraph.*

Gilbert Parker. THE TRANSLATION OF A SAVAGE. By GILBERT PARKER, Author of ' Pierre and His People,' ' Mrs. Falchion,' etc. *Crown 8vo. 6s.*

'The plot is original and one difficult to work out; but Mr. Parker has done it with great skill and delicacy. The reader who is not interested in this original, fresh, and well-told tale must be a dull person indeed.'—*Daily Chronicle.*

'A strong and successful piece of workmanship. The portrait of Lali, strong, dignified, and pure, is exceptionally well drawn.'—*Manchester Guardian.*

'A very pretty and interesting story, and Mr. Parker tells it with much skill. The story is one to be read.'—*St. James's Gazette.*

Gilbert Parker. THE TRAIL OF THE SWORD. By GILBERT
PARKER, Author of ' Pierre and his People,' etc. *Crown 8vo. 6s.*
A historical romance dealing with a stirring period in the history of Canada.

Arthur Morrison. TALES OF MEAN STREETS. By ARTHUR
MORRISON. *Crown 8vo. 6s.*

' Told with consummate art and extraordinary detail. He tells a plain, unvarnished
tale, and the very truth of it makes for beauty. In the true humanity of the book
lies its justification, the permanence of its interest, and its indubitable triumph.'—
Athe

' Each story is complete in itself, vivid, engrossing. His work is literature, and
literature of a high order.'—*Realm.*

'A great book. The author's method is amazingly effective, and produces a thrilling
sense of reality. The writer lays upon us a master hand. The book is simply
appalling and irresistible in its interest. It is humorous also ; without humour
it would not make the mark it is certain to make.'—*World.*

' Mr. Morrison has shot the flashlight of his unmistakable genius. The literary
workmanship is of the highest order.'—*Aberdeen Press.*

' Powerful pictures from the lower social depths.'—*Morning Post.*

Robert Barr. IN THE MIDST OF ALARMS. By ROBERT
BARR, Author of ' From Whose Bourne,' etc. *Crown 8vo. 6s.*

' A delightful romance with experiences strange and exciting. There are two pretty
girls in the story, both the heroes fall in love, and the development of this thread
of the tale is in all respects charming. The dialogue is always bright and witty ;
the scenes are depicted briefly and effectively ; and there is no incident from first
to last that one would wish to have omitted.'—*Scotsman.*

Pryce. TIME AND THE WOMAN. By RICHARD PRYCE,
Author of ' Miss Maxwell's Affections,' ' The Quiet Mrs. Fleming,'
etc. New and Cheaper Edition. *Crown 8vo. 6s.*

' Mr. Pryce's work recalls the style of Octave Feuillet, by its clearness, conciseness,
its literary reserve.'—*Athenæum.*

Marriott Watson. DIOGENES OF LONDON and other
Sketches. By H. B. MARRIOTT WATSON, Author of ' The Web
of the Spider.' *Crown 8vo. Buckram. 6s.*

' By all those who delight in the uses of words, who rate the exercise of prose above
the exercise of verse, who rejoice in all proofs of its delicacy and its strength, who
believe that English prose is chief among the moulds of thought, by these
Mr. Marriott Watson's book will be welcomed.'—*National Observer.*

Gilchrist. THE STONE DRAGON. By MURRAY GILCHRIST.
Crown 8vo. Buckram. 6s.

' The author's faults are atoned for by certain positive and admirable merits. The
romances have not their counterpart in modern literature, and to read them is a
unique experience.'—*National Observer.*

THREE-AND-SIXPENNY NOVELS

Edna Lyall. DERRICK VAUGHAN, NOVELIST. By
EDNA LYALL, Author of ' Donovan,' etc. *Crown 8vo. 3s. 6d.*

Baring Gould. ARMINELL : A Social Romance. By S.
BARING GOULD. *New Edition. Crown 8vo. 3s. 6d.*

Baring Gould. URITH: A Story of Dartmoor. By S. BARING GOULD. *Third Edition.* *Crown 8vo.* 3s. 6d.

'The author is at his best.'—*Times.*
'He has nearly reached the high water-mark of "Mehalah."'—*National Observer.*

Baring Gould. MARGERY OF QUETHER, and other Stories. By S. BARING GOULD. *Crown 8vo.* 3s. 6d.

Baring Gould. JACQUETTA, and other Stories. By S. BARING GOULD. *Crown 8vo.* 3s. 6d.

Gray. ELSA. A Novel. By E. M'QUEEN GRAY. *Crown 8vo.* 3s. 6d.

'A charming novel. The characters are not only powerful sketches, but minutely and carefully finished portraits.'—*Guardian.*

J. H. Pearce. JACO TRELOAR. By J. H. PEARCE, Author of 'Esther Pentreath.' *New Edition.* *Crown 8vo.* 3s. 6d.

A tragic story of Cornish life by a writer of remarkable power, whose first novel has been highly praised by Mr. Gladstone.
The 'Spectator' speaks of Mr. Pearce as '*a writer of exceptional power*'; the 'Daily Telegraph' calls the book '*powerful and picturesque*'; the 'Birmingham Post' asserts that it is '*a novel of high quality.*'

Clark Russell. MY DANISH SWEETHEART. By W. CLARK RUSSELL, Author of 'The Wreck of the Grosvenor,' etc. *Illustrated.* *Third Edition.* *Crown 8vo.* 3s. 6d.

X. L. AUT DIABOLUS AUT NIHIL, and Other Stories. By X. L. *Crown 8vo.* 3s. 6d.

'Distinctly original and in the highest degree imaginative. The conception is almost as lofty as Milton's.'—*Spectator.*
'Original to a degree of originality that may be called primitive—a kind of passionate directness that absolutely absorbs us.'—*Saturday Review.*
'Of powerful interest. There is something startlingly original in the treatment of the themes. The terrible realism leaves no doubt of the author's power.'—*Athenæum.*
'The stories possess the rare merit of originality.'—*Speaker.*

O'Grady. THE COMING OF CUCULAIN. A Romance of the Heroic Age of Ireland. By STANDISH O'GRADY, Author of 'Finn and his Companions,' etc. Illustrated by MURRAY SMITH. *Crown 8vo.* 3s. 6d.

'A flashlight thrown on the greatness and splendour of our ancestors. Redolent of freshness and purity.'—*Cork Herald.*
'The suggestions of mystery, the rapid and exciting action, are superb poetic effects.'—*Speaker.*
'For light and colour it resembles nothing so much as a Swiss dawn.'—*Manchester Guardian.*
'A romance extremely fascinating and admirably well knit.'—*Saturday Review.*

Constance Smith. A CUMBERER OF THE GROUND. By CONSTANCE SMITH, Author of 'The Repentance of Paul Wentworth,' etc. *New Edition.* *Crown 8vo.* 3s. 6d.

Author of 'Vera.' THE DANCE OF THE HOURS. By the Author of 'Vera.' *Crown 8vo.* 3s. 6d.

Esmè Stuart. A WOMAN OF FORTY. By Esmè Stuart, Author of 'Muriel's Marriage,' 'Virginie's Husband,' etc. *New Edition. Crown 8vo.* 3s. 6d.
'The story is well written, and some of the scenes show great dramatic power.'—*Daily Chronicle.*

Fenn. THE STAR GAZERS. By G. Manville Fenn, Author of 'Eli's Children,' etc. *New Edition. Cr. 8vo.* 3s. 6d.
'A stirring romance.'—*Western Morning News.*
'Told with all the dramatic power for which Mr. Fenn is conspicuous.'—*Bradford Observer.*

Dickinson. A VICAR'S WIFE. By Evelyn Dickinson. *Crown 8vo.* 3s. 6d.

Prowse. THE POISON OF ASPS. By K. Orton Prowse. *Crown 8vo.* 3s. 6d.

Grey. THE STORY OF CHRIS. By Rowland Grey. *Crown 8vo.* 5s.

Lynn Linton. THE TRUE HISTORY OF JOSHUA DAVIDSON, Christian and Communist. By E. Lynn Linton. Eleventh Edition. *Post 8vo.* 1s.

HALF-CROWN NOVELS

A Series of Novels by popular Authors, tastefully bound in cloth.   2/6

1. THE PLAN OF CAMPAIGN. By F. Mabel Robinson.
2. DISENCHANTMENT. By F. Mabel Robinson.
3. MR. BUTLER'S WARD. By F. Mabel Robinson.
4. HOVENDEN, V.C. By F. Mabel Robinson.
5. ELI'S CHILDREN. By G. Manville Fenn.
6. A DOUBLE KNOT. By G. Manville Fenn.
7. DISARMED. By M. Betham Edwards.
8. A LOST ILLUSION. By Leslie Keith.
9. A MARRIAGE AT SEA. By W. Clark Russell.
10. IN TENT AND BUNGALOW. By the Author of 'Indian Idylls.'
11. MY STEWARDSHIP. By E. M'Queen Gray.

12. A REVEREND GENTLEMAN. By J. M. COBBAN.
13. A DEPLORABLE AFFAIR. By W. E. NORRIS.
14. JACK'S FATHER. By W. E. NORRIS.

Other volumes will be announced in due course.

Books for Boys and Girls

Baring Gould. THE ICELANDER'S SWORD. By S. BARING GOULD, Author of 'Mehalah,' etc. With Twenty-nine Illustrations by J. MOYR SMITH. *Crown 8vo. 6s.*

A stirring story of Iceland, written for boys by the author of 'In the Roar of the Sea.'

Cuthell. TWO LITTLE CHILDREN AND CHING. By EDITH E. CUTHELL. Profusely Illustrated. *Crown 8vo. Cloth, gilt edges. 3s. 6d.*

Another story, with a dog hero, by the author of the very popular 'Only a Guard-Room Dog.'

Blake. TODDLEBEN'S HERO. By M. M. BLAKE, Author of 'The Siege of Norwich Castle.' With 36 Illustrations. *Crown 8vo. 3s. 6d.*

A story of military life for children.

Cuthell. ONLY A GUARD-ROOM DOG. By Mrs. CUTHELL. With 16 Illustrations by W. PARKINSON. *Square Crown 8vo. 3s. 6d.*

'This is a charming story. Tangle was but a little mongrel Skye terrier, but he had a big heart in his little body, and played a hero's part more than once. The book can be warmly recommended.'—*Standard.*

Collingwood. THE DOCTOR OF THE JULIET. By HARRY COLLINGWOOD, Author of 'The Pirate Island,' etc. Illustrated by GORDON BROWNE. *Crown 8vo. 3s. 6d.*

'"The Doctor of the Juliet," well illustrated by Gordon Browne, is one of Harry Collingwood's best efforts.'—*Morning Post.*

Clark Russell. MASTER ROCKAFELLAR'S VOYAGE. By W. CLARK RUSSELL, Author of 'The Wreck of the Grosvenor,' etc. Illustrated by GORDON BROWNE. *Second Edition, Crown 8vo. 3s. 6d.*

'Mr. Clark Russell's story of "Master Rockafellar's Voyage" will be among the favourites of the Christmas books. There is a rattle and "go" all through it, and its illustrations are charming in themselves, and very much above the average in the way in which they are produced.'—*Guardian.*

Manville Fenn. SYD BELTON : Or, The Boy who would not go to Sea. By G. MANVILLE FENN, Author of 'In the King's Name,' etc. Illustrated by GORDON BROWNE. *Crown 8vo. 3s. 6d.*

'Who among the young story-reading public will not rejoice at the sight of the old combination, so often proved admirable—a story by Manville Fenn, illustrated by Gordon Browne? The story, too, is one of the good old sort, full of life and vigour, breeziness and fun.'—*Journal of Education.*

The Peacock Library

A Series of Books for Girls by well-known Authors, handsomely bound in blue and silver, and well illustrated. Crown 8vo. 3/6

1. A PINCH OF EXPERIENCE. By L. B. WALFORD.
2. THE RED GRANGE. By Mrs. MOLESWORTH.
3. THE SECRET OF MADAME DE MONLUC. By the Author of 'Mdle Mori.'
4. DUMPS. By Mrs. PARR, Author of 'Adam and Eve.'
5. OUT OF THE FASHION. By L. T. MEADE.
6. A GIRL OF THE PEOPLE. By L. T. MEADE.
7. HEPSY GIPSY. By L. T. MEADE. 2s. 6d.
8. THE HONOURABLE MISS. By L. T. MEADE.
9. MY LAND OF BEULAH. By Mrs. LEITH ADAMS.

University Extension Series

A series of books on historical, literary, and scientific subjects, suitable for extension students and home reading circles. Each volume is complete in itself, and the subjects are treated by competent writers in a broad and philosophic spirit.

Edited by J. E. SYMES, M.A.,
Principal of University College, Nottingham.

Crown 8vo. Price (with some exceptions) 2s. 6d.

The following volumes are ready :—

THE INDUSTRIAL HISTORY OF ENGLAND. By H. DE B. GIBBINS, M.A., late Scholar of Wadham College, Oxon., Cobden Prizeman. *Fourth Edition.* With Maps and Plans. 3s.

'A compact and clear story of our industrial development. A study of this concise but luminous book cannot fail to give the reader a clear insight into the principal phenomena of our industrial history. The editor and publishers are to be congratulated on this first volume of their venture, and we shall look with expectant interest for the succeeding volumes of the series.'—*University Extension Journal.*

A HISTORY OF ENGLISH POLITICAL ECONOMY. By L. L. PRICE, M.A., Fellow of Oriel College, Oxon.

PROBLEMS OF POVERTY: An Inquiry into the Industrial Conditions of the Poor. By J. A. HOBSON, M.A. *Second Edition.*

VICTORIAN POETS. By A. SHARP.

THE FRENCH REVOLUTION. By J. E. SYMES, M.A.

PSYCHOLOGY. By F. S. GRANGER, M.A., Lecturer in Philosophy at University College, Nottingham.

THE EVOLUTION OF PLANT LIFE: Lower Forms. By G. MASSEE, Kew Gardens. With Illustrations.

AIR AND WATER. Professor V. B. LEWES, M.A. Illustrated.

THE CHEMISTRY OF LIFE AND HEALTH. By C. W. KIMMINS, M.A. Camb. Illustrated.

THE MECHANICS OF DAILY LIFE. By V. P. SELLS, M.A. Illustrated.

ENGLISH SOCIAL REFORMERS. H. DE B. GIBBINS, M.A.

ENGLISH TRADE AND FINANCE IN THE SEVENTEENTH CENTURY. By W. A. S. HEWINS, B.A.

THE CHEMISTRY OF FIRE. The Elementary Principles of Chemistry. By M. M. PATTISON MUIR, M.A. Illustrated.

A TEXT-BOOK OF AGRICULTURAL BOTANY. By M. C. POTTER, M.A., F.L.S. Illustrated. 3s. 6d.

THE VAULT OF HEAVEN. A Popular Introduction to Astronomy. By R. A. GREGORY. With numerous Illustrations.

METEOROLOGY. The Elements of Weather and Climate. By H. N. DICKSON, F.R.S.E., F.R. Met. Soc. Illustrated.

A MANUAL OF ELECTRICAL SCIENCE. By GEORGE J. BURCH, M.A. With numerous Illustrations. 3s.

THE EARTH. An Introduction to Physiography. By EVAN SMALL, M.A. *Illustrated.*

INSECT LIFE. By F. W. THEOBALD, M.A. *Illustrated.*

Social Questions of To-day

Edited by H. DE B. GIBBINS, M.A.

Crown 8vo. 2s. 6d.

2|6

A series of volumes upon those topics of social, economic, and industrial interest that are at the present moment foremost in the public mind. Each volume of the series is written by an author who is an acknowledged authority upon the subject with which he deals.

The following Volumes of the Series are ready :—

TRADE UNIONISM—NEW AND OLD. By G. HOWELL, M.P., Author of 'The Conflicts of Capital and Labour.' *Second Edition.*

THE CO-OPERATIVE MOVEMENT TO-DAY. By G. J. HOLYOAKE, Author of 'The History of Co-operation.'

MUTUAL THRIFT. By Rev. J. FROME WILKINSON, M.A., Author of 'The Friendly Society Movement.'

PROBLEMS OF POVERTY: An Inquiry Into the Industrial Conditions of the Poor. By J. A. HOBSON, M.A. *Second Edition.*

THE COMMERCE OF NATIONS. By C. F. BASTABLE, M.A., Professor of Economics at Trinity College, Dublin.

THE ALIEN INVASION. By W. H. WILKINS, B.A., Secretary to the Society for Preventing the Immigration of Destitute Aliens.

THE RURAL EXODUS. By P. ANDERSON GRAHAM.

LAND NATIONALIZATION. By HAROLD COX, B.A.

A SHORTER WORKING DAY. By H. DE B. GIBBINS and R. A. HADFIELD, of the Hecla Works, Sheffield.

BACK TO THE LAND: An Inquiry into the Cure for Rural Depopulation. By H. E. MOORE.

TRUSTS, POOLS AND CORNERS: As affecting Commerce and Industry. By J. STEPHEN JEANS, M.R.I., F.S.S.

THE FACTORY SYSTEM. By R. COOKE TAYLOR.

THE STATE AND ITS CHILDREN. By GERTRUDE TUCKWELL.

WOMEN'S WORK. By LADY DILKE, MISS BULLEY, and MISS WHITLEY.

Classical Translations

Edited by H. F. FOX, M.A., Fellow and Tutor of Brasenose College, Oxford.

Messrs. Methuen propose to issue a New Series of Translations from the Greek and Latin Classics. They have enlisted the services of some of the best Oxford and Cambridge Scholars, and it is their intention that the Series shall be distinguished by literary excellence as well as by scholarly accuracy.

Crown 8vo. Finely printed and bound in blue buckram.

CICERO—De Oratore I. Translated by E. N. P. MOOR, M.A., Assistant Master at Clifton. 3s. 6d.

ÆSCHYLUS—Agamemnon, Chöephoroe, Eumenides. Translated by LEWIS CAMPBELL, LL.D., late Professor of Greek at St. Andrews. 5s.

LUCIAN—Six Dialogues (Nigrinus, Icaro-Menippus, The Cock, The Ship, The Parasite, The Lover of Falsehood). Translated by S. T. IRWIN, M.A., Assistant Master at Clifton; late Scholar of Exeter College, Oxford. 3s. 6d.

SOPHOCLES—Electra and Ajax. Translated by E. D. A. MORSHEAD, M.A., late Scholar of New College, Oxford; Assistant Master at Winchester. 2s. 6d.

TACITUS—Agricola and Germania. Translated by R. B. TOWNSHEND, late Scholar of Trinity College, Cambridge. 2s. 6d.

CICERO—Select Orations (Pro Milone, Pro Murena, Philippic II., In Catilinam). Translated by H. E. D. BLAKISTON, M.A., Fellow and Tutor of Trinity College, Oxford. 5s.

Methuen's Commercial Series

BRITISH COMMERCE AND COLONIES FROM ELIZABETH TO VICTORIA. By H. DE B. GIBBINS, M.A., Author of 'The Industrial History of England,' etc., etc. 2s.

A MANUAL OF FRENCH COMMERCIAL CORRESPONDENCE. By S. E. BALLY, Modern Language Master at the Manchester Grammar School. 2s.

COMMERCIAL GEOGRAPHY, with special reference to Trade Routes, New Markets, and Manufacturing Districts. By L. D. LYDE, M.A., of The Academy, Glasgow. 2s.

COMMERCIAL EXAMINATION PAPERS. By H. DE B. GIBBINS, M.A. 1s. 6d.

THE ECONOMICS OF COMMERCE. By H. DE B. GIBBINS, M.A. 1s. 6d.

A PRIMER OF BUSINESS. By S. JACKSON, M.A. 1s. 6d.

COMMERCIAL ARITHMETIC. By F. G. TAYLOR, M.A. 1s. 6d.

A FRENCH COMMERCIAL READER. By S. E. BALLY. 1s. 6d.

9 783337 366209